Groundbreaking! The Conscious Bride *is one of those rare books that can change the way we view a common event like the wedding. It is an invaluable resource, not only for brides, but for anyone seeking to understand the wedding journey.*

—Robert A. Johnson, leading Jungian analyst and best-selling author of *She: Understanding Feminine Psychology* and *We: Understanding the Psychology of Romantic Love*

When women are trying to cope with a problem, struggling through a major life transition, or just in need of a reality check and a little healing support, we go straight to our friends. Each of the books in the *Women Talk About* series reflects the experiences of dozens of women from diverse backgrounds, whose words are accompanied by provocative insights from the latest research. Often funny, sometimes painful, and always honest, their powerful voices reassure us that we're not alone, offer guidance and wisdom, and show us how to connect back to the woman we want to be.

The
Conscious
Bride

Women Unveil Their True Feelings about Getting Hitched

Sheryl Nissinen

New Harbinger Publications, Inc.

Publisher's Note

This publication is designed to provide accurate and authoritative information in regard to the subject matter covered. It is sold with the understanding that the publisher is not engaged in rendering psychological, financial, legal, or other professional services. If expert assistance or counseling is needed, the services of a competent professional should be sought.

Distributed in the U.S.A. by Publishers Group West; in Canada by Raincoast Books; in Great Britain by Hi Marketing, Ltd.; in South Africa by Real Books, Ltd.; in Australia by Boobook; and in New Zealand by Tandem Press.

Cover design by Blue Design
Edited by Heather Garnos
Text design by Michele Waters

Library of Congress number: 00-134877
ISBN 1-57224-213-2 Paperback

Printed in the United States of America

New Harbinger Publications' Web site address: www.newharbinger.com

04 03

10 9 8 7 6 5 4

To my circle of women—Jessica, Carrie, and Danielle.

To my grandparents, Charlotte and Isidore Brustein,
for their love and wisdom.

Contents

Chapter One

The Whole Story   1

A Lifetime Commitment ❦ The Wedding's Shadow ❦
Rites of Passage: The Three Phases of Transition ❦ Trying
to Deny Our Experience ❦ You Are Not Alone ❦ Two
Roadmaps: Ancient and Modern Mythologies

Chapter Two

Cutting the Ties That Bind   27

Rites of Separation ❦ The Proposal ❦ The Engagement
Ring ❦ Circle of Friends: Separating from Girlfriends ❦
Leaving the Nest: Separating from Mother ❦ No Longer
Number One: Separating from Father ❦ Loss of Identity:
Separating from the Identity as a Single Woman

Chapter Three

The Quest for Perfection   71

The "Perfect" Defense ❦ A Mythological and Spiritual
View ❦ The Wedding Dress ❦ The Princess and the
Queen ❦ Slowing Down ❦ Dropping into Being

Chapter Four

Has Everyone Gone Mad?   **97**
> The Wedding as Theater 🌾 Daddy's Little Girl: Bride and
> Father 🌾 The Modern Aphrodite: Bride, Groom,
> Mother-in-Law 🌾 That Stepmother 🌾 Maids of Honor
> 🌾 Bride and Groom 🌾 The Final Weeks 🌾 Rites of
> Separation Revisited: Separating from Fiancé

Chapter Five

The Wedding Day   **131**
> A Microcosm of Life 🌾 The Wedding: A Day of
> Transition 🌾 Pan Rears His Head: From Chaos to
> Serenity 🌾 From the Reception to the Wedding Night

Chapter Six

The First Year   **165**
> Rites of Incorporation: Becoming a Wife 🌾 The Wedding
> Lasts a Day—the Marriage, a Lifetime 🌾 Postbridal
> Depression: Another Wedding Shadow 🌾 What Is a Wife?
> 🌾 The "I" Within the "We" 🌾 The One-Year Anniversary

Chapter Seven

A New Vision of Marriage   **197**
> A Guiding Vision 🌾 Examining Our Expectations 🌾 A
> Creative Endeavor 🌾 A Love Letter

Recommended Reading   **213**

Notes   **215**

References   **217**

Acknowledgements   **219**

Chapter One

The Whole Story

I had a sense right away that I would marry him. It was a very fast courtship. We fell deeply in love very quickly—it wasn't a When Harry Met Sally thing at all! There was a sense that this is "the one" even though I don't believe that there is only one person out there. There was a change in me when I met him. I knew that I wanted to spend the rest of my life with him. And I didn't even believe in marriage when we met!

—Vivian

Every time I expressed a negative emotion to anyone they would say, "Are you sure you want to get married? Are you having doubts?" It was like any emotion besides pure joy led them to believe that I was having doubts. I knew in every fiber of my being that this was the man with whom I was meant to spend the rest of my life—but did that mean I wasn't allowed to have any difficult feelings before making the biggest commitment I had ever made?

—Paulina

I feel alone. People ask me about the arrangements but not about how I feel. I'm not sure they really understand, even my fiancé. So even though I have all these people helping me, I still feel isolated. I haven't talked about how I really feel with anyone.

—Carmen

A Lifetime Commitment

Congratulations! If you are holding this book in your hands, it is because you have recently become engaged. Either a proposal was offered to which you responded with a "Yes!" or you decided together that it was time to take the next step and move your commitment toward marriage. The two of you have been brought together by a deep love, the special bond that only you share, and it is your loving bond that has led you to this unique point in your life. Your love has inspired you to create a wedding that will reflect the beauty and devotion that surrounds the two of you at the highest moments of your time together. The engagement signifies the promise you have made to meet each other at the altar and publicly declare your commitment.

There are few occasions in life more beautiful and awe-inspiring than a wedding. When two people decide to solidify their commitment, they begin the sacred journey of marriage, which begins with the engagement and continues through the rest of their lives. Today, in most cases, marriage is no longer a legal contract entered into to secure the economic well-being of both parties, nor is it a social obligation imposed upon two individuals to secure the bonds between their families. As the sexes become more equal, we no longer *need* to marry for the reasons that have determined this union for centuries. Yet the fact remains that we still *want* to marry. We want to make a lifetime commitment to the one person who has encircled our hearts and affected our lives like no one else.

If marriage is no longer a legal, economic, or social obligation, what leads people to marry? Today, it seems we enter marriage for one reason: to love—to grow through love, to explore the possibilities of love with one person, to bring children into a home full of love. And it seems that this impulse to explore love's possibilities as a married couple is evident nearly the moment we meet our future life partner. Almost every woman with whom I spoke while writing this book acknowledged a sense of "knowing" very early in the relationship that they had met the person with whom they would spend the rest of their lives. Jade reflected: "I just knew, I don't know how else to explain it. We were together eight years before we married but I knew the first day I saw him that I would marry him." Brenda, married to her husband for over twenty years, said:

I knew almost from the moment I first met him. I was reading tea leaves in the college cafeteria and he came over and had his leaves read, and I saw that this was the man that I would be with for the rest of my life.

Even those women who don't believe in the popular notion of "soul mates" felt this sense of uncanny knowing. Vivian said:

I had a sense right away that I would marry him. It was a very fast courtship. We fell deeply in love very quickly—it wasn't a When Harry Met Sally *thing at all! There was a sense that this is "the one" even though I don't believe that there is only one person out there. Something about our relationship was different. It was the first time in my life that I didn't throw in the towel when it wasn't working out. There was a change in me when I met him. I knew that I wanted to spend the rest of my life with him. And I didn't even believe in marriage when we met!*

From this strong love, the desire to marry is born. For many couples the impulse to marry seems to bypass their rational, analytical mind. They feel as if they are being led by something beyond thought to sanctify and formalize their love and commitment to one another. As you may have already noticed within your own engagement, when a couple decides to marry, an ancient and powerful pattern of energy comes into play; we could say that the *wedding archetype*, or model, helps guide the couple through the engagement, into the wedding day, and through the first year of marriage. For some, their engagement is a joyous time filled with planning and animated discussion about their wedding day and future life together. For most, however, the engagement is a combination of excitement, stress, bliss, and confusion. The roots of the excitement and happiness are clear; it is the stress and confusion of this time that have been ignored.

The road that leads to and from the wedding day is not always smooth. The moment the declaration is made to enter into a lifetime commitment, a wide array of difficult emotions rises to the surface. In other words, the engagement, wedding, and first months of marriage can be a difficult time where one person in the partnership—usually the one more aligned with her feminine nature—feels overwhelmed by emotions and forces that she has never experienced and does not understand. (This book is geared toward the bride, but in some cases it may be the groom who is more in touch with his feminine nature, or his internal cycles of death and rebirth.) As a culture we carry the misconception that two people can marry without any psychological preparation as individuals. Bride and groom are expected to plan a "perfect" day and arrive at this day feeling serene and ready to commit to a lifetime partnership. Yet they are offered little guidance on how to create this inner serenity. Women are generally bewildered by the energy that consumes them in the months prior to their wedding. As Diana said, "This one event had total control over me. I felt enslaved by something I didn't understand."

If the wedding is to achieve its main function, which is to bring together two individuals into one marriage, then both members of the union deserve to know what is happening internally before their wedding day. Through reading this book you will explore the reasons behind the common tendency for women to "freak out" at some point during their engagement, wedding, and/or first year of marriage. You will be given the opportunity to deepen the bliss and beauty of the process as well as explore the difficult emotions that have, for the most part, been silenced. You will also be offered a context in which to understand the profound transformation that begins within one or both partners from the moment they decide to marry.

Throughout the book I will refer to "marriage" and "the bride," but feel free to replace these words with terms that work for you. Because what we are talking about is an archetype, it makes no difference what we call this commitment—marriage, sacred union, spiritual partnership; it makes no difference what combination of races, cultures, and sexes enter into this union—a Catholic man and a Jewish woman, an African-American woman and a Caucasian man, two women; it makes no difference whether the wedding consists of three people or three hundred people. What matters is the intention to make a lifetime commitment and the basic human pattern that leads to this commitment. So although the book is largely written for heterosexual couples, the energy that consumes "brides" applies to all committed unions. When we view the wedding this way we remove its veils and return it to its rightful place as an important rite of passage in adult life.

The Wedding's Shadow

My marriage, like all marriages, began with the wedding. And like romantic love, the wedding journey, from the engagement to the wedding day and through the first year of marriage, was filled with as much darkness as light. If, before my engagement, someone had told me that this would be so, I would not have believed her. I had been culturally conditioned to view the wedding only as a day of untarnished joy. I had come to believe that to feel fear or sadness at any time in the wedding process indicated that there was something wrong with our relationship. The images in the magazines, films, and advertisements I had seen portrayed beautiful, blissful brides smiling like princesses on their wedding day. Never once did I encounter an image or article that expressed the dark side of the event. During my wedding journey I realized that the loss, confusion, and depression that live in the wedding's underbelly have been excluded from the bridal affair.

It was the confusion that surfaced during my engagement that inspired me to begin the research that eventually led to this book. The confusion began nearly the moment my husband first proposed to me. I had been waiting, quite impatiently, for many months to hear those words, "Will you marry me?," but when they finally arrived I found myself retreating. This slight withdrawal came in the form of distaste for the ring with which he proposed, and it was only much later that I learned that it is very common to displace uncomfortable feelings onto tangible objects. In fact, this tendency to transfer our fear, anger, anxiety, grief, madness, and confusion onto more concrete things like the wedding dress, the flowers, and the caterer often characterizes the wedding experience. Because we do not know that we are allowed to feel anything "negative" about the wedding, we try to ignore these feelings. But, as I quickly learned, feelings cannot be ignored, and if they are not brought to light they will make themselves known in other ways.

Feeling grief and anger and utterly confused about my experience, I made my way toward my wedding day. Despite these difficult feelings, I never once doubted that this was the man I was meant to marry. We had both known from nearly the moment we met that we would spend the rest of our lives together, and this sense of certainty about our commitment remained unshakable. But then why did I feel so anxious and confused? Attempting to understand what was happening to me, I searched bookstores, libraries, and the Internet, and while I certainly found plenty of information on the planning end of the wedding— shelves lined with guides on how to plan the perfect event, entire books dedicated to the cake, and magazines that flaunted gorgeous, flawless brides on their covers—I found almost nothing on the psychological and emotional aspects involved in the process. I knew that I was undergoing a profound spiritual transformation, one that involved a change of identity, yet nowhere did I find the information that would help me make sense of this experience. It was during these months that the seeds for this research took root. I read, I talked with other brides, I researched, I wrote, I dreamed . . . until the plant broke ground and the information contained in this book was born.

Through my discussions with other women, I learned that I was not alone in my confusion. Whenever I told women that I was researching the "dark" underbelly of the wedding journey, I was nearly unanimously met with exclamations of relief: "You mean I'm not the only one to have experienced anything less than perfect bliss around my engagement and wedding?!" And on the heels of this thought they often lowered their voice to a tone that reflected the belief that they were violating one of our culture's greatest myths: that the wedding is supposed to be a pure, perfect day. The women with whom I spoke came from diverse cultural, religious, racial, sexual, and socioeconomic backgrounds. They lived in various parts of the country and ranged in age from twenty-three to fifty-two. What they all shared was the sense that there are large gaps in what is being talked about when it comes to the wedding. They were befuddled by the range and intensity of feelings that accompanied every phase of their wedding journey. Some had searched for information and come up empty-handed; others had attempted to stifle what they felt should not exist.

Almost all the women felt disappointed by at least one aspect of the wedding itself when it fell short of their expectation of how they thought it "should" have been. Our culture sets up powerful images for how a wedding should look. From the time we are young children, we are inundated with images of fairy-tale weddings and beautiful brides resplendent in their gowns. We have watched as chiseled men propose in elaborate, creative ways to their teary-eyed girlfriends, always placing that perfect diamond on her elegant finger. We have swooned when the fireworks explode on the wedding night, illuminating the blissed-out newlyweds in their rose-petal bridal bed. There is nothing harmful about these images within themselves. Many women *are* swept off their feet by the proposal and they *do* experience a slice of perfection on their wedding day. But these experiences represent only half the story. What about the tension that escalates between the family members as the wedding day nears? What about the exhaustion that commonly consumes both bride and groom on their wedding night and precludes any thought of a romantic union? Sophia summed up her wedding experience a year after the event:

The clash between fantasy and reality resulted in many stark disappointments around my wedding. Basically, my proposal, wedding day, wedding night, honeymoon, and first year of marriage were nothing like I thought they were going to be. I looked forward to each of these events with tremendous excitement, only to find myself profoundly confused by the sense of loss, aloneness, and depression that colored each of them. Emotionally, nothing proceeded as expected.

Herein lies the wedding's shadow, for as brightly as the images of the perfect wedding shine, so do they cast a shadow of equal intensity. We know we cannot have light without shadow, yet somehow we have avoided confronting this shadow when it comes to discussing weddings. It is as if all the shadow aspects of the wedding—those elements deemed inappropriate by our culture—have been tucked within the taffeta of the bridal gowns or concealed within the decorative frosting on the cake. The one-sided image of the wedding process that we see in the media furthers the illusion that weddings are only about joy, happiness, and laughter. Of course brides feel joyous and excited as their special day approaches, but these emotions are often joined by fear and grief. In a culture that glorifies the wedding day as the pinnacle of joy in a woman's life, brides try to sweep these darker emotions aside. They feel that there is no place for them at the wedding.

As we will explore in depth in chapter 4, when brides feel the wedding energy beginning to possess them, they quickly funnel this energy into the only concrete avenue our culture offers: the planning. They believe that if they follow the traditional template for planning a wedding—checking off their lists of things to do in their appropriate time frame—they will glide onto their wedding day with serenity.

Yet many of the women felt cheated by our culture's emphasis on the planning to the exclusion of emotional assistance. As Helen stated one month before her wedding:

My fiancé and I have both been engaged before. He's forty-five and I'm thirty-two and this was a first marriage for both of us, so we were ready to get married. We planned a short engagement—three months. I love to plan parties and have planned many of them before, so I didn't think it would be any problem to plan our wedding in a short time span. But what no one told me is that it's not the planning that is so stressful, it's the emotional roller-coaster I've been on. Everyone says, "It takes a year to plan a wedding"—and now I know why. It takes a year to allow the emotions to move through you; it takes a year to adjust to the concept of committing yourself to one person; it takes a year to allow time and space for the fear, the anxiety, the numbness, and the sadness to work themselves out. Three months is too short for a major psychological transformation to occur. Transformations take time. At first I thought there was something wrong with me for having these feelings, but then I realized that they are part of the transformation. These are the things that no one talks about, probably because they haven't put them into words themselves.

Women who had been married thirty years were just as relieved as young women on the cusp of marriage to learn that there was nothing "wrong" with them for feeling sadness, anger, depression, and confusion around the time of their wedding. In fact, not only were their feelings normal and expected, but they were a *necessary* part of the inner transformation that is generated by the wedding.

Rites of Passage:
The Three Phases of Transition

This book is based on the premise that the wedding is a rite of passage, and that all rites of passage—adolescence, the wedding, the birth of a child, a geographic move, a job change, midlife, old age—involve a transformation of *identity* as the initiate sheds the old way of life and makes way for the new role. In 1960, a Dutch anthropologist named Arnold van Gennep introduced into Western culture the term "rite of passage" to describe these transitions. Through studying various groups of indigenous people, he observed: "The life of an individual in any society is a series of passages from one age to another and from one occupation to another. . . For every one of these events there are ceremonies whose essential purpose is to enable the individual to pass from one defined position to another which is equally well defined" (3).

Van Gennep observed that the process of crossing from one position to another was divided into three phases: rites of separation, transition rites, and rites of incorporation. In regard to the wedding, the woman *separates* from her family of origin and her identity as a single woman during her engagement; shortly before the wedding and as a bride she enters a *transition* period, or liminal phase, where she is in an in-between state; and in the first year of her marriage she *incorporates* her identity as wife and completes the joining with her husband. (All of these phases are explored in depth in later chapters). In indigenous cultures, the initiate is carefully guided through these three phases by the elders of the society. Through a series of well-defined and ancient rituals, the members are then able to transition into the next phase of their development. Indigenous cultures understand that one cannot endure these passages alone.

When brides are given a context in which to understand what is happening to them, they are given full permission to feel all of their feelings as they arise. When a woman understands that during her engagement she is supposed to feel sadness as she relinquishes an identity that she has held her entire life, fear about the magnitude of the commitment she is about to enter, perhaps a little bit of anger at the man who is taking her away from the life she has always lived, and numbness as she folds in her wings and creates an internal quiet space inside which she can endure this transformation—then she is free to move into her new identity as wife without the excess baggage of her singlehood. On the other hand, when women attempt to squeeze themselves into the corset of how they think they should be feeling, they often feel as if they are going out of their minds. As Diana said:

I didn't know who I had become. I felt as if I were possessed by a demonic force that had its grip around my neck. I was a mad woman, screaming at people who hadn't sent RSVPs on time, lashing out at my mother and sister, obsessing about the tiniest details of the wedding. It was only much later that I realized that all of that was because I refused to feel the loss inherent to this event.

When brides understand the function of each phase of transition, the emotions that accompany each phase can be allowed expression in their pure, unadultered form. Without the need to hide or contort itself into a more acceptable form, grief is simply grief. But faced with the obligation to wear a certain mask, grief turns into guilt, anger smolders into shame, and fear transforms into madness.

It is no wonder that brides often feel lost and alone during this transition. Our culture doesn't provide the necessary ceremonies that honor all rites of passage. We are expected to become adolescents, wives, fathers, and elders without the traditions of ritual, dance, music, and insight that should accompany these transitions. This results in a culture where individuals may struggle with the unfinished residue from the previous role, which can inhibit progression into the next phase of life. It also creates a sense of aloneness as we are left to make sense of changes without the guidance of our elders. Alone and in the absence of ritual, it is common for brides to face the enormity of the transition behind the shield of denial. We, as a culture, are not aware that endings and losses need to be grieved. When we express sadness about an event that "should" be positive—graduating from high school, a wedding, moving to a new city—we are often met with the ultimate phrase of denial, "Look on the bright side." Often the unfinished transitions of our childhood and adolescence come together at a major life event like the wedding. As Sophia wrote:

The transition into marriage activated all of the unfinished transitions that had accumulated in my life. I realized that I had become an adolescent without grieving my childhood, and an adult without the necessary rituals that would release me from my ties to adolescence, so within the role of adult I carried within me the old identities of child and adolescent. I had passed through significant rites of passage—the onset of menstruation, losing my virginity, college graduation—without the knowledge that I was passing through a phase of life. Each half-finished transition carried residue into the next passage until finally, with the wedding, I crumbled under the weight of so much tattered emotion.

Women need to know that in becoming engaged, they begin a rite of passage, a challenging time that carries within it the potential for tremendous inner growth. As a woman relinquishes her ties to her current identity, she learns how to surrender and let go. As she incorporates her new identity as wife, she is offered a chance to decide who she will become within this new role. The time in between two identities is a precious, vulnerable time—a blank space where all opportunities arise. The bride may experience sadness from other losses in her life; she may grieve other unfinished transitions, as Sophia did. It is a time when she can clean out her inner house so she can meet her husband on solid ground. Beyond any list of external tasks to complete, the most important task for the bride is to attend to her thoughts and feelings. Checking off the boxes on the to-do lists will not, in itself, ensure a serene day. When brides, grooms, and their families are given full permission to experience "what is" and move through all three phases of this transition with consciousness, they can arrive at the wedding day and begin the marriage with self-awareness, resolution, and serenity.

Trying to Deny Our Experience

It is impossible to grieve and let go if we have refused to invite grief and surrender to our wedding experience. Although the rite of passage of the wedding beckons brides to break down so they can build themselves anew, most women adamantly attempt to hide and avoid these breakdowns. Psychoanalyst Marion Woodman (1985) commented on this phenomenon: "Many people are being dragged toward wholeness in their daily lives, but because they do not understand initiation rites, they cannot make sense of what is happening to them. They put on a happy face all day, and return to their apartment and cry all night" (24).

Why do we feel that we must deny our true experience? One explanation is that when it comes to the wedding, we are bombarded by the need to "put on a happy face all day." As stated earlier, the message of our society is that the wedding and all that surrounds it, including the engagement and the first year, is to be only a happy time. In fact it epitomizes the Western value of revering the positive—happiness, harmony, joy, beauty—and concealing all that we conceive as negative—anger, grief, death. Brides are suctioned into this mind-set the moment they decide to marry. It causes them to think that there is something wrong with their relationship if they experience anything less than pure joy during this time, which then leads them to hide their true experience, even from themselves. In fact, this belief is so entrenched that in casual conversation many brides had difficulty admitting that their wedding included any dark spots. It was only when we closed the office door and I explained the healthy context in which I understand the wedding process that the women breathed the "I'm not the only one" sigh of relief and gratefully shared their story. As Paulina said:

Every time I expressed a negative emotion to anyone they would say, "Are you sure you want to get married? Are you having doubts?" It was like any emotion besides pure joy led them to believe that I was having doubts. I knew in every fiber of my being that this was the man with whom I was meant to spend the rest of my life—but did that mean I wasn't allowed to have any difficult feelings before making the biggest commitment I had ever made?

The women with whom I spoke who had been married several years and were far past the point of equating a difficult wedding period with a faulty marriage expressed the sentiment, "I wish I had had this information when I got married. It would have saved me a lot of agony." When a bride tries to deny her true feelings, they either shoot out externally into the planning or implode into her body (or a combination of both). In the first case, the bride becomes manic around the planning and in the latter case the emotions affect her physical body. As Sophia wrote:

About six months before my wedding, I started having all these terrifying symptoms, like having a hard time eating and breathing. I had no idea what was happening to me and I felt like there was no one I could talk to about it. I remember that some of the physical symptoms were alleviated by writing in my journal about my fears of loss and abandonment, issues related to my mother, and my fear of losing my husband. Mostly I remember feeling terrified. I felt like I was dying. My instinct told me that this was related to the wedding, but the intensity of the fears made no sense in the context of how we usually view this event.

In fact, although it may sound extreme, Sophia was aligned with the first phase of her rite of passage, and seen within this context, her fears made perfect sense. If a rite of passage is to be complete, it must involve a letting go, a shedding, a separation, indeed, the *death* of the old identity before the new identity and the new life can take hold. During the wedding the woman transforms from maiden to wife, and just as a caterpillar cannot transform into a butterfly without completely ceasing to be a caterpillar, so a woman cannot grow into a wife without sacrificing herself as maiden. In an indigenous culture, or a culture that honored community and ritual, Sophia would have been guided through her transition on the arms of her village elders, grandmothers, mother, sisters—all who had passed that way before. She may still have felt as if she were dying, but she would not have been terrified by this sensation. The emotions spawned by her rite of passage would have been contained by rituals and ceremonies that were meticulously designed to guide her into her next phase of life and her identity as wife. Yet we are expected to become wives automatically, without any guidance to help us through this critical rite of passage.

How is it that we are denied the guidance and consciousness that many cultures consider a birthright? Here we turn to one of the basic creeds that dominates Western culture: the inability to allow death to occupy its rightful patch in the quilt of daily living. The ceremonies involved in rites of passage assume a worldview where death is invited to participate actively. Death—and its circle of intimate sisters which include surrender, loss, and sacrifice—informs the psychological and spiritual life of indigenous cultures. Rites of passage involve a rite of death and a rite of rebirth: a dying of the old status or identity and a birth into the new. In this manner, ritual and death are forever intertwined. Therefore, to understand this lack of ritual is to confront the cultural denial of death. To view the wedding as a rite of passage, we must invite this hidden shadow into the picture.

This may feel frightening to you, as it will for many in our culture who see death only as the great specter that one encounters with the final breath. Viewed in this light, as something separate from life and concentrated into a single, isolated event, it is understandable that people often turn from it with horror. Without witnessing loss as it appears in small moments throughout the day—in the letting go of hands, in the falling of leaves, in the coming apart of bodies, in the shedding of blood each month—psychological death becomes equated with literal death. Yet it is important to understand that the loss involved in a rite of passage is a *metaphoric* death, or a shedding of identity. It is a necessary loss that opens the space for new life, a letting go of the single aspect of oneself and making room for the married wife. As Dana commented:

Before and immediately after my wedding I felt like I was dying—and every cell of my body felt like that was what was happening. There was no convincing it otherwise. It was almost like a visceral experience. I had to keep reminding myself that this was part of the transition and that it would not always be like this. I had to remind myself what I know about cycles of nature: that just as spring always follows winter, an internal death is always, always followed by a rebirth.

Death is only scary if we do not believe that new life will arrive. In the context of the wedding, we can rest assured that not only will new vitality be infused into the bride and groom, but that the light they will feel in the months after their wedding will shine with greater intensity and clarity the more they are able to grieve their losses of identities and ways of life during the engagement.

Unfortunately, most brides keep their difficult feelings at bay during the engagement. But eventually, usually on the wedding night, honeymoon, or sometime in the early months of marriage, the bride will crumble. The darker emotions will make themselves known and insist on being reckoned with. A typical scenario is the bride who cries in her hotel room on her wedding night. She either attempts to shield the tears from her husband, or the poor groom looks on feeling helpless and confused. If he asks why she cries, most likely she will not know. Both women and men deserve to know what is happening to them, for without an understanding of the big picture, even the joy of the wedding day can be overwhelmed by untamed emotion.

You Are Not Alone

"I feel so alone," brides often express in the months before their wedding. They share that even though they are surrounded and assisted by friends, family, and their groom, they still feel alone with their wedding experiences. As Carmen said eight months before her wedding:

I feel alone. People ask me about the arrangements but not about how I feel. I'm not sure they really understand, even my fiancé. So even though I have all these people helping me, I still feel isolated. I haven't talked about how I really feel with anyone.

Because brides tend to feel hemmed in by the ramifications of the wedding's shadow, they attempt to silence the feelings they think should not exist. This creates an even greater feeling of aloneness, not only within themselves in that they are cut off from their feelings, but the less brides talk about the true wedding experience, the more this confirms the illusion that they are alone with their less-than-blissful emotions. Internally, brides are yearning to connect with others who can understand what they are experiencing during this time. Part of the aloneness that women feel comes from the fact that, because the wedding casts such a vast shadow, many people are not aware that a bride may be feeling anything other than happiness during her engagement. As Dana said:

I was very aware of this allegory about the wedding, that it's supposed to be a "white picket fence" day, but that's not what it was for me at all. I felt very alone with my true feelings of confusion and distress because so many people didn't understand, they didn't want to cop to it, talk about it, or address it. I felt that I was left to make sense of it alone.

Helen had a similar experience:

I was just saying to my fiancé this morning, "Wouldn't it be nice if there was anyone we could sit down with and talk about how strange this is—who would say, "Yeah, it is strange."? The truth is that I've started doing that because I've needed to be honest about my experience. When people ask, "How's it going with the wedding?" I say, "The planning is going great but you wouldn't believe all this other emotional work, and no one talks about it anywhere!"

Furthermore, because the focus in our culture is on the details of the planning, people just don't think to ask the bride what she's feeling. Like Helen, Jade felt dismayed by this reality:

Weeks before our wedding we met with our reverend. He had us talk about why we loved each other, when we fell in love, what love means to us. He was the only one that asked us, "Are you guys ready for this? Are you aware of what this means? What kinds of feelings have you been having?" Everyone else was concerned with: "So what are you wearing? What are your bridesmaids wearing?" The people around the bride need to probe deeper before she gets married.

Jade felt relieved that one objective person asked her about her relationship and emotional life. Her desire was that all who were close to her—mother, friends, brothers, aunts, stepfather—would gather around to protect and guide her through her rite of passage. Instead, quite the opposite occurred: one day she looked around and saw that everyone had become engaged in their own wedding drama. This tendency toward high drama can lead many brides to feel isolated—not only feeling alone with the internal world of their emotional transformations but also that the drama of the wedding lies solely on their shoulders. The bride is often expected to deal with the problems that arise with blended families, spurned girlfriends, and the mother-in-law who wants to control the entire affair.

There is no question that the wedding process does create quite a spectacular drama. It invites a host of classic characters to visit particular scenes and asks the bride to change characters many times throughout the play. Brides may be relieved to know that the future mother-in-law's disdain for the bride, the mother's fierce attachment to her daughter, the protective father, and the stepmother who does not receive an invitation to the affair are all scenes that have been acted out repeatedly throughout the drama of human history. Oftentimes when people live outside of community and isolated within a fragmented circle of friends, they are denied the opportunity to witness their dramas on the larger, universal stage. This can exacerbate the sense of aloneness the bride already feels and create a disconnection from the whole fabric of human stories. It is important for brides to know that they are far from alone with their emotions, their thoughts, and their wedding dramas.

Two Roadmaps: Ancient and Modern Mythologies

Nowhere can we find the depiction of universal dramas more than in myths. Myths, like fairy tales, are stories that are born of the collective experience of an entire era and culture. They are like a roadmap to the human psyche in that they offer psychological insight into the things that are true for all people. Linking our personal story to the great web and patterns of those who have traveled that path before can significantly alleviate the aloneness and confusion that often plague the modern woman. Myths show us what our stories have in common. They can help us sort through our experience by offering time-honored psychological solutions to common problems. Brides may be especially comforted to learn that their modern anxiety is echoed by women who lived over two thousand years ago. The larger-than-life dramas that consume the bride can be brought down to human scale when she learns that each step of her journey is a common, necessary part of her transformation into becoming a wife, and that each step has been walked by millions of brides before.

One myth that clearly shows the processes and trials through which a bride passes during her initial transition from maiden to wife is the compelling Greek myth of Psyche and Eros. This myth tells of a beautiful young woman named Psyche (meaning "soul") who, at the start of our story, is tied to Death mountain, thinking she will be married to Death. Instead she finds herself married to Eros, the god of love. Eros' task is to kill the beautiful Psyche, who is a threat to his mother, Aphrodite, the goddess of love and beauty (notice the classic theme of the jealous mother-in-law!). But instead of killing her, he accidentally falls in love with her. In order to be allowed to marry Eros, Psyche must follow Aphrodite's orders and complete four impossible tasks. I will refer to this myth at various points throughout the book to illustrate specific aspects of the bride's passage. (For a complete understanding of the myth and a clear interpretation of how it parallels the process of women's psychological growth, please see Robert Johnson's *She: Understanding Feminine Psychology*).

For some people, ancient myths provide the missing link in their understanding of their life paths. But, for others, ancient myths can be difficult to grasp. Our modern minds are not accustomed to listening to the telling of an experience in terms of symbols and metaphors. We like to hear it told like it is. So while mythology can provide an ancient psychological roadmap, the fact remains that women need to hear the stories of other living, modern women during the crucial wedding transition. We need to know that we are not alone with the multitude of emotions and experiences that fill our days. As women, we are nourished by the sharing of common experiences; our soul breathes a sigh of relief when we learn that other women share our thoughts, obsessions, and emotions. Without community, we believe that we're the only one having this experience; the feelings then become entrenched, reducing the possibility of recognizing and expressing them.

In tribal communities, no one endures a rite of passage alone. The initiate is carefully guided by all who have passed through the rites before. She is attended to at each phase of her passage, enfolded in the arms of the women in her community. But as Westerners we live so much of our lives isolated within the shells of single family homes, cars, and solitary desks. Hungry for community, we often turn to television, movies, magazines, and computers to connect to others through the sharing of a common experience. While these avenues do provide some sense of validation, they generally tell of surface experience and do not reach into the depths of the psyche where we can be touched by the fresh tears and the real ramblings of others.

Today most of us do not live in a community that can provide this connection. Even if we have a close circle of girlfriends, chances are we have migrated to other parts of the state, country, or even world. Not only have we lost touch with the psychological mythologies that cultures around the globe have relied on for centuries, but we have lost the modern mythologies created by women living in close quarters who gather for tea or lemonade and discuss every aspect of their lives in minute detail. This book can be utilized as a piece of modern wedding mythology. It is a collection of women talking about every phase of the wedding journey, from their first feelings the moment they heard the words "Will you marry me?" into the joys and disappointments of the wedding day and through the depression, questioning, and peacefulness of the first year of marriage. When woven together, the words can provide a tapestry for a woman to gaze upon when she feels alone and confused by her wedding, gaining awareness and comfort by sharing in the multilayered journeys of women who have passed this way before.

Chapter Two

Cutting the Ties That Bind

There are certain images that make me almost break down when I think of them. One is when we walk down the aisle and my dad lets go of my hand, then sits behind me as I walk up to the altar. I will feel the loss in that act. I mean, that's it, that's the separation.

—Kelsey

I feel like I'm jumping off a cliff and wondering when I start walking on the bottom who I'm going to become. It feels like such a transformation. I've been acting strange, much more introverted, quiet. It's like I can't feel myself and I can't feel my love for my fiancé. I said to him the other day, "I just want you to know that I'm not normally who I've been in the last month and a half."

—Helen

It was very important for me to keep my last name. I didn't associate it with anything political or social; it was a way of hanging on to myself, to my identity. I didn't want to create a new identity as his wife in such an explicit way. It would have pushed me over the edge into unreality if I went from Diana Hansen to Diana Lutz. I felt like I surrendered so much of my identity in this process that to do that would have felt like I was bordering on having no identity base at all. I had had my name for thirty-seven years and I saw no reason to give that up too.

—Diana

Rites of Separation

The engagement marks the beginning of a woman's moving away from her identity as a single woman and her primary allegiance to her family and moving toward the identity of a wife and the new union with her husband. Ultimately, to solidify this bond with her groom, she must begin to sever ties with those who helped form and mold her as a young woman. The engagement, besides being a time to plan the wedding day, is also a time when a woman is separating psychologically from her girlfriends, mother, and father, as well as from her current identity as a single woman. This first phase of the wedding rite of passage is what van Gennep called rites of separation.

The Proposal

The process of moving into the identity of wife begins with the proposal. It is at that moment, when a woman responds affirmatively, that she becomes linked to another in a way that previously existed only with friends and family. Many women felt the impact of the proposal seconds after the word "yes" was spoken. Some were ecstatic; others felt that with this tiny exchange of dialogue the change of identity had begun. The feelings elicited were a confusing combination of loss and excitement. Diana, now married six years, described her proposal:

I was having a really bad day. I was actually disgusted with myself and was taking off my clothes, tossing them around the room, telling my boyfriend that I was feeling really sad. I crawled into bed and he came and got in with me. I don't really remember the details of what happened next, except that he handed me the ring with the idea that the question was implicit in the diamond ring. I was confused. I asked him what it was and he said, "It's an engagement ring." I had no feeling in my body. I think it didn't make sense to me that he was asking me to marry him, so I just felt numb. I went into the bathroom and closed the door and cried. What it felt like was that when I put the ring on my finger I moved from Diana, single in the world, to now belonging to somebody, and the ring was emblematic of being brought in, enfolded, enfolded by him. It felt very surreal. But I was also thrilled and excited. I was in my mid-thirties and somebody I loved was actually asking me to marry him! It was such a confusing mix of emotions.

Other women felt pure joy after the proposal. It met their expectations and they felt delighted by the entire event. Isabel talked about her proposal:

Oh, my proposal was so romantic! He completely surprised me by flying me to the Napa Valley. He had purchased different outfits for me and I could choose which one to wear. All he said was that he was taking me for a surprise. We arrived and got to a beautiful bed-and-breakfast that was hidden in the woods. It was gorgeous. All he said was that I had to be up very, very early in the morning. I had no idea what was going on. So at 4:30 A.M. a car came and picked us up and took us to a field where a limo came and took us to another field. He said that we were going on a hot air balloon ride and I thought, "How romantic." It was one year to the day that he said "I love you," so that's what I thought we were celebrating and this was my gift. His plan was to propose on the hot-air balloon but when he started fidgeting to get the ring I said, "Oh, just hold me. Let's enjoy this moment together." So I wouldn't let him propose when he wanted to! When we landed we were taken to this gorgeous garden where they had a table set up with flowers and a bottle of champagne. A man came with a guitar and said he would be playing music for me today. I still had no idea about the proposal and just said, "Oh okay. How sweet!" Marcus decided to recite one of my favorite poems. He had tears in his eyes. Then he got down on one knee and asked me in Spanish if I would be his wife. Of course I said yes immediately. I was so happy. Some people were watching from the distance and everyone was crying! It was so romantic. My engagement is one of the most precious moments of my life. I will cherish it always.

Isabel's proposal was like a fairy tale. Her husband, Marcus, is a traditional romantic, to the point where "what he would have ideally wanted was to take me to a castle and propose to me like Prince Charming. He wanted this ideal, romantic, dreamlike thing." In fact, the proposal far exceeded the media-driven expectations that have seeped into our subconscious minds as to what a proposal "should" look like. On some level, living in this culture, most of us carry clear images of how this first wedding step should look, and if the external circumstances or our inner world fail to live up to these images, we wonder if there is something wrong with us or our relationship. While many proposals are romantic, equally as many are casual and even disappointing. Vivian's husband, Jared, proposed while they were driving home from a dinner party—she said "It was a horrible proposal!" What stood out most for her was the feeling that with this exchange of words her identity change had been set into motion:

*I was completely in shock. Shocked that he proposed
when he did, how he did. I felt like it was out of my
control. I don't think of myself as a controlling person,
but there was this sense that with four words—will you
marry me—I had already started this process of losing my
identity and getting married and I felt like I had been
excluded from the decision because he had proposed. I had
two tumultuous days. I wouldn't let him call anybody to
tell them that we were engaged because I had to absorb
it, I just couldn't believe it. I wasn't sure that I wanted it
to happen right then. I made myself have a hard look at
my emotions. Soon I realized that, yes, this was something
I had wanted but now that it was happening I was
fighting it.*

Women felt confused by the tradition of the man asking the question. Some women, even self-proclaimed feminists, felt it was important that the man ask the question, yet
they wanted it done their way and within their time frame!
They struggled with conflicting desires: On the one hand,
even though they were aware that the tradition is somewhat
outdated and archaic, they could not shake the deeper
impulse to abide by it; on the other hand, they could not
wait passively and allow the man to determine the timing of
a decision that would equally affect both of them. Sophia
wrote about her struggle around this issue:

*Mikael and I had been together around eight months when
I suddenly felt consumed by a strong desire for him to
propose to me. And with Christmas fast approaching, my
fantasy mind tirelessly imagined the different scenarios:
would it be Christmas Eve, in front of the fire, with the
perfect diamond solitaire placed at the bottom of the
champagne glass? Or perhaps he would pull me onto his
lap early Christmas morning, reveal the small, black velvet*

box, and whisper the magic words into my ear. Whatever the scene, I was sure that it would be well planned and thoroughly romantic.

But my husband did not propose on Christmas. Nor did he propose on New Year's Eve nor on Valentine's Day. As the typical proposal days passed, an anger began to brew inside me. Suddenly my inner feminist was unleashed: Why should I wait passively for him to propose? Why does the timing of a decision that equally involves me rest in his hands? I felt out of control and attempted to regain a modicum of control by arguing with tradition. Yet when I would pose these questions to my not-quite-fiancé and he would suggest that I ask the question, I vehemently refused. I wanted him to ask the question, but I wanted it done my way and on my timetable! We became entrenched in a power struggle in which he felt controlled and he reacted with resistance. He ended up proposing on our living room floor on a Thursday evening—a far cry from the proposal I had imagined. I was still ecstatic, but within that happiness there was a palpable disappointment. We've been married four years now and we have just now understood the underlying dynamics in the issue. It was actually a disappointment for both of us.

Many couples bypass the waiting game that comes with this traditional role-playing and instead decide together that they want to marry. While this approach may dampen some of the romance, it also reflects the equality in today's relationships and honors the impulses and desires of each partner. Angela commented:

I think romance is about intimacy and honest communication. Samuel and I had been together a couple of years and were taking our favorite hike when suddenly the topic felt right to talk about. I think we had both been feeling for some time that yes, we wanted to marry, we wanted to take the next step. I had actually brought it up about six months earlier and he said that he wasn't ready to talk about it yet. That was hard, because I felt like I was waiting on him, but I had to respect that and just back off and trust. So on the hike I brought it up and we talked it through, and then he said, "Will you marry me?" We were both laughing and I said, "Yes, of course." As soon as we said it out loud we felt like the world dropped away. We stood holding each other on top of the mountain and knew that our decision was guided by something deeper, and that it was our decision. It was one of the most honestly romantic moments of my life.

This is not the typical proposal we see portrayed in films and television. It is important to know that proposals come in all shapes and sizes and that one is no better than any other. Of the women I spoke with, about a third of the proposals were traditionally romantic; a third were casual and disappointing; and another third of the couples decided together to marry and there was no formal proposal at all. More importantly, the degree of romance and creativity in the proposal has absolutely no bearing on the success or failure of the marriage. This directly contradicts the unspoken message we receive from our culture, which says that the depth of the man's love is determined by the extent to which he plans and executes his proposal: "the more creative and romantic the proposal, the more he loves me." The inaccuracy of this message is exemplified by Daniela, whose boyfriend stopped traffic on the Golden Gate Bridge to get down on one knee and propose to her; a year after the wedding they were divorced.

The Engagement Ring

With a formal proposal comes an engagement ring, which symbolizes the first stage of union—a beautiful public statement that says, "We have made a promise to be wed." It speaks of the way the man sees his partner and the way that he feels she sees herself. The diamond, in its brilliance and purity, is representative of the core maiden self, the most innocent aspect that lives inside a woman. It is Psyche, the pure and virginal dewdrop, the maiden before she is transformed into a queen. Today men propose with a wide variety of jewels and styles, but no matter what kind of ring he proposes with, the ring is the first concrete object representing their eternal union. Brides talked about the significance of their engagement ring and how they felt when they first received it. Like the proposal, the feelings around the ring ranged from delighted to disappointed, and everything in between.

Carmen: *I was shocked by the ring. It was a big ring and I was expecting a smaller diamond. This is the biggest ring I have ever had and it felt like I was announcing to the world that I am engaged. I think that slight hesitation reflected that I realized that things had changed. After I got engaged things would never be the same as they once were. I think that's what I was afraid of. A friend at work helped convince me that the ring was beautiful, but I still sat down with my fiancé and asked if he would be hurt if I exchanged it. I did not exchange it, and I am so glad. He put his heart and a lot of thought into the ring. I love it now. It is a constant reminder of his love for me and of the commitment we will make in eight months.*

Anna: *My husband did not propose with a ring at all. I never had an engagement ring, which was sad for me. He's just not that type of guy, and that's part of what I have learned to accept about him.*

Paulina: *I love my ring. It is a perfect diamond and it makes me feel like a princess when I look at it. It is pure and clear, just like our love.*

Diana: *I was very disappointed in the ring. It didn't look like the ring I would have imagined being given. It was small and . . . well ... ugly. It was a small, ugly ring that didn't seem to have anything to do with me, with who he knew me to be. I would have expected a beautiful, clear, square cut, chiseled ring that announced itself. But this ring was puny. I felt like the ring belonged to somebody else. I felt misunderstood. It felt like something he had bought at a pawn shop or something that he had once given somebody else and just happened to have lying around and now was giving to me—you know, it just had that feeling to it. It didn't feel like a statement of love. It felt embarrassing for me to wear it. I was profoundly disappointed. I felt that the ring must have been emblematic of the whole thing, the unrealness of it all.*

Remember Isabel, with the fairy-tale, hot air balloon proposal? The difficult issues around her engagement ring continued into the second year of her marriage:

He proposed with a gorgeous ring that was everything I told him I didn't want. When we knew we were going to get married we had a conversation about the ring and I said I wanted something very simple and understated. And he got something beautiful but not necessarily simple and not necessarily understated! My preference was platinum and I got gold. To this day it continues to be an issue.

We've talked a lot about it. Everyone says, "What's your problem with it? You're crazy. Any woman would love to have a ring like that." I have so many people complimenting me on the ring everywhere I go. However, those who know me say, "That's definitely a beautiful ring but it's not you. It's not what you would have chosen."

This is a subject that I cannot discuss with a lot of people because they look at the ring and think it's gorgeous, and it is. But that wasn't the issue. The issue was to be able to go and pick the ring with him, or have some kind of say in the ring that I'm going to wear for the rest of my life, which is a symbol of my marriage. We had a session with our therapist about my wanting to return the ring, but Marcus was not receptive to it. He took it very personally. Now he's ready, years later, to consider changing the setting or getting another ring. At this phase we're ready to do that, but back then we weren't ready.

Through many discussions about it, Isabel and Marcus discovered that Marcus validated himself through the ring. He wanted to give her what he thought was the best ring possible. He wasn't listening to what Isabel had to say. Marcus said he was old-fashioned, that he wanted to be able to choose the ring and surprise Isabel with it. When she asked him why he didn't hear that she wanted platinum, he said, "I like gold on your skin." This has been an ongoing issue between them that they have only recently resolved by Isabel finding the ring that she wants.

Isabel thought she was the only one to feel disappointed about her ring and was both relieved and surprised to learn that other women have misgivings about the ring with which their fiancé proposed. Rebecca said, "I didn't like the ring my fiancé gave me. I knew that he had put thought into it but it just wasn't me. We went to exchange it the next day for something that I wanted." Isabel's and Rebecca's feeling that they should have a say in the ring that they would wear for the rest of their lives reflects the changing course of today's marriages. We no longer live in an age where the man comes to the bride's father's house to ask for his daughter's hand in marriage, then sweeps her off her feet, carries her into his home, and provides for her financially. Even for those couples who do abide by this traditional economic model the marriage often includes an emotional and psychological equality that has been emerging between the sexes for the last thirty years. As Isabel astutely commented, we may need to modify our traditions to reflect these significant changes. For many women it feels intolerable to allow the man to decide what ring she will wear on her hand for the rest of her life. While some women ended up exchanging the ring that the man proposed with for something that they loved, others felt that they had to "learn to love it," but that it was not the ring they would have chosen for themselves. For far too many centuries, women have had to silence their true needs and desires and defer to those of the man—and men have carried the burden of having to guess which ring their fiancée will love. This unnecessary pressure weighs heavily on both partners.

Some women decided to do away with the whole tradition of the engagement ring. They felt it signified ownership and wanted nothing to do with the history of female subordination that marriage has represented. They said that wearing a ring would have been a statement that they had given in to the traditional suburban-wife-serves-husband model. These were usually the same women who kept their maiden name and balked against a formal proposal. Brenda, married over twenty years, remembered how she felt about her ring in 1969:

When he first gave me the diamond engagement ring I almost flushed it down the toilet. I felt confused because I was happily moving so far away from the middle class, Jewish, suburban life and the ring seemed to represent all that. Todd didn't even want to give me the ring but I wanted it. But then when I had it I felt like, "What does this mean about who I am?" It didn't fit with the hippie world in which I was defining myself.

Brenda's statement reflects the struggle that women go through around many aspects of the wedding: They feel drawn to abide by traditional customs—wearing a white wedding dress, taking the man's last name—yet do not want to conform to the meaning embedded into those customs. Since the 1960s, feminists have bemoaned the rings—both engagement and wedding—because of their resemblance to links in a chain, thus the connotations of being "chained" to or enslaved by a man. There is some truth to this since the origins of marriage derive from patriarchal concepts of ownership, and some women refuse the ring for this valid reason. Yet it seems that we, as modern women, are being called to redefine the meaning of these traditional items in a way that reflects our current ideologies. We are being asked to reconcile the conflicting urges that propel us into following these traditions while at the same time making it clear that we do not conform to the meaning that these symbols have always held. What determines an object's meaning is the meaning we ascribe to it. In this way, the meaning can change over time and depending on who interprets the objects. As relations between men and women have evolved, so has our understanding of marriage, the wedding, and the tangible items that symbolize the intangible feelings spawned by the bridal process. Sara redefined the ring's meaning based on a symbolic understanding of precious metals, circles, and jewels. Two months before her wedding she said:

I understand my engagement ring to signify a promise to meet my fiancé at the altar and sanctify our commitment. The circle represents the never-ending nature of union; the platinum represents the durability of our commitment; and the diamond reflects the shining, glimmering love that entered my life when we met. There is something so pure, almost untouchable about my ring. It is like a slice of perfection on my finger. When I look at it, it reminds me of my promise to always aspire to be all I can be, for my own sake as well as for the marriage. I have to say, though, that when I first wore it I felt slightly bound, claustrophobic. I had never worn a ring on any finger, so there was the physical aspect of having something on me all the time that was not so easy to take off. I felt a little trapped by it. Every time I looked at it I got butterflies—from excitement and from fear. I realized a few months later that I must have also felt scared by the concept of this lifetime commitment, and that part of this fear was put onto the ring. I don't feel that anymore. The ring is like a body part. I feel naked when I take it off.

The ring, preceded by the proposal, is the first step in the engagement process—a process that is, paradoxically, one of union *and* separation. When a woman looks at her ring she is reminded not only of the beauty of the love between herself and her beloved but also of the part of herself that she is relinquishing in order to join with this man, as seen in Sara's comment. There is an aspect of the proposal that is like an abduction, a way in which the woman is captured by the man and thus begins the process of her initiation. When she resists the ring it could be because she already feels the loss of her singlehood beginning. As much as she had been longing to hear those words and see that ring upon her finger, any unconscious resistance she has to the marriage process is initially transferred onto the ring.

From the moment she puts the ring on her finger, the journey into marriage begins. Regardless of what our particular understanding is of the proposal and ring, the decision to marry begins the woman's rites of separation.

Circle of Friends:
Separating from Girlfriends

Often the process of separation begins with one's girlfriends and/or sisters, especially those that have been a part of the bride's life since childhood. Even if the bride's friends are already married, they often represent the life that she is leaving: the innocence of childhood, the struggles of adolescence, the independence of young adulthood. A bride may find herself reminiscing about her past with her friends or daydreaming about a certain period of her life when she felt particularly free. In the months before her wedding, Sophia daydreamed about her early years at college when she was living in the dormitories. She felt that that period in her life symbolized an emerging independence when she was responsible to no one but herself. With her marriage, she would give up a large degree of that solitude and freedom. The separation can also result in the bride clinging tighter to her friends and sisters during this period, again resisting the abduction as she senses that marriage will temporarily remove her from their world, or the world they represent, and alter her relationship with them. The ropes are strengthened before they are cut and tied back together with a different knot.

However, while she moves toward them, she needs to realize the full implications of what it means to separate: As she leaves their world and the life of a single woman, she will experience a certain restraint on her freedom. Marriage, in most cases, means the commitment to physical fidelity, as well as another sort: harnessing the energy previously directed toward the opposite sex and focusing it on one person "for as long as you both shall live." It means realizing the difference between being unattached and being married, between being single and being a wife. Judith S. Wallerstein and Sandra Blakeslee, in their book *The Good Marriage: How and Why Love Lasts*, expand on this notion: "Another aspect of separation is ending the self-absorption of adolescence and young adulthood. As one woman remarked to me, 'Suddenly I realized I wasn't playing anymore. There's a real person at the other end of this who might get hurt.' Even in young adulthood we are protected by our adolescent sense of timelessness, by the ease with which we can assume and discard a role . . . and by a sense of unreality. At marriage the young woman moves into the unknown" (56).

It is important to acknowledge the transition away from the carefree nature of adolescence and singlehood. Our bridal showers and bachelorette parties attempt to celebrate one last time the woman's singlehood, but more often than not they fail to create a safe space for the bride to explore her emotional and psychological state. The traditional bridal shower where the woman receives lingerie and cookware does little to assist the bride with her transition. True to many aspects of the wedding, it focuses on the external feminine needs to the exclusion of the inner world. Jade described an urge to connect with the women around her in the weeks and months before the wedding and was disappointed by the trivial nature of her shower:

Everyone got me lingerie and I was like "Huh?" It was not what I was needing. It was great to have all those women in one room, but not to play games. I would have wished for something more spiritual. I would have loved to have gone away somewhere and had a more contemplative experience.

Victoria's shower did succeed in creating a safe space for her to explore her singlehood and her friendships. Two of her girlfriends organized a weekend in a beautiful, secluded retreat center in the wilderness with the intention of surrounding Victoria with rituals that would reflect the changing course of her identity. Six of her girlfriends and her sister flew in from all parts of the country to "shower" one of their closest friends. Victoria describes the weekend as one of the highlights of her whole wedding experience. The weekend included a lot of girl talk and games, hiking, sitting in the hot tub, and cooking, but the real bonding occurred during the evening ritual that her best friend had planned. In our modern age, women often find that creating rituals of their own satisfies their yearning for community and guidance. Aspects of Victoria's ritual can be used as a blueprint for creating meaningful bridal showers. She described the ritual in detail and what it meant to her:

We were a little nervous about the ritual because I'm open to ceremony and being honest in a group, but some of the girls are a little more reserved. We didn't know if it would work. We sat in a circle, some on the couch, some in chairs, lit candles, invoked a small prayer, and began. It was a talking ritual, meaning that the format was to pose three questions, one at a time, and allow people to speak their mind on each subject. We did it in a talking stick fashion, which is derived from a Native American tradition. The way it works is the stick, which can be any item, is placed in the middle, and whoever wants to speak next picks it up. The guidelines are: Speak from the heart. Listen from the heart. Do not interrupt when someone else is speaking. May your words be lean and concise. Nothing leaves the circle without permission. We used a red velvet scrunchy that my mom made for me as the talking stick! It was neat because of course everyone held it as they talked so it got charged with all that energy. I remember and feel all my girlfriends every time I wear it.

The first question was: What are your thoughts and views on marriage? What does marriage mean to you? What does that word mean to you? What images does it conjure up? Everyone spoke one at a time. It was great for me to hear all the different perspectives on marriage and check my own assumptions against them. In the group we had one divorced woman, one married woman, and one woman who was possibly going to get married for legal, immigration reasons (to keep her boyfriend in the country). So everyone came from their unique perspective and gave their reflections. We don't think about what marriage means to us until we're about to get married, so it was great for everyone to explore the topic. It was something we kept coming back to all weekend—in the pool and hot tub, on hikes. It was so good for me to explore it to that degree with all my girlfriends.

The second question was: Does anyone have any fears about how their relationship with me might change after the wedding? This was an important question because it honored my friends and gave them the space to talk about their feelings. Once the real wedding frenzy began there would be no room for their fears, feelings, wants, and needs to be expressed. I wanted to know if they were afraid of losing me or something changing. And people spoke! They had a lot to say! They were afraid I might lose myself because my husband has such a strong personality, but they were also afraid that they would lose me. They encouraged me to do whatever I could to keep my independence—doing things like keeping my own voice mail or going away with them for the weekend felt important to them. They didn't want to lose that. They wanted to feel like they could have their own relationship with me separate from my husband at times. I expressed that I wanted that too but that I also wanted them to be open, especially in the beginning, that when I came to visit I might have my husband with me. I wanted them to connect with me in his presence as much as they could, and connect with him.

This was their time to focus on their relationship with me as Victoria Hill. It had come out that I was changing my name to Victoria Jackson. The change felt very significant and tangible and unfamiliar—like, who was Victoria Jackson going to be and what will that mean? Some of these girls had known me as Vicky Hill for twenty-six years. I was twenty-eight when I got married and twenty-seven at the bridal shower. I had known two of these girls from age two, another from age seven, another age eleven, another age eighteen, my sister my whole life, and only one for a year. So people had serious old attachments to who I had always been and who I had been to them. People were crying. It was very emotional. I could feel that on some level they were letting go of these attachments. I didn't know why we were crying exactly. There was a lot of sadness there, and so much love.

The third question was: How had my love affected them? This could be seen as a setup to give me my praises, but it felt appropriate. Here I was devoting myself to love through marriage and it was neat to hear how my love had affected them. It was nice to know, before leaping into this lifelong commitment of marriage, that I had some skills at loving. This part just blew me away. I felt completely humbled by the end, and still do when I think about it. One friend said I had taught her about her feelings; another said I had taught her about love; another said I had taught her about stability and commitment. Everyone said such profound, beautiful, impactful things.

The ritual was three hours long. We were all exhausted. If you look at the pictures of the shower everyone had red noses and red eyes from crying. We didn't drink a drop of alcohol. There wasn't a stripper on board. If there was a stripper it was the stripping of protection. If there was revealing it was the revealing of truth and love. The ritual was completely intense and profound, so special and truthful. At the end I needed my own space so I didn't sleep in the group with all the women. They had poured so much love into me, it was so raw, that I knew I had to take it in by myself. I also knew that after the wedding day I would be without them and I needed to know how to go through a huge ritual and then curl up within and take care of myself. I knew that I needed that practice, to let go of their hands after being so close and going through something transformational together.

The next morning we had breakfast, took hikes, and swam. We kept returning to the topics that we had discussed the night before but in a more casual way. And then it was over. We all said goodbye and drove back to the city. The next time we would be together was on the wedding weekend. But I felt so fed by the bridal shower weekend that I could feel them with me for the next two months, even though they were thousands of miles away.

Victoria's shower provides a beautiful model for an alternative to the traditional "lingerie and cookware" party. She felt enfolded and deeply nourished by her girlfriends in a way that allowed her more room to move forward with the wedding planning. She said that she often thought about her shower when she needed strength and emotional, feminine sustenance: "the shower weekend filled me with a calm that accompanied me through the wedding day." It also served her on her wedding day in that all her bridesmaids had shared a bond and were able to gather more closely around her. There was no time at the wedding to explore their changing friendships, and there was no need to do so. The shower not only helped Victoria—it also helped her girlfriends to negotiate the shifts in their friendship. As Victoria said, it gave them the space to vocalize their concerns and fears about the changes brought on by her marriage. Because they were encouraged to thoroughly express these fears and thoughts, they did not need to be redirected onto things like the planning. Victoria did not experience the common arguments that flare up between the bride and her girlfriends around planning issues because the underlying feelings had been deeply and honestly addressed.

And yet, while it is wonderful to feel the bond between women strengthen before the wedding, it is important that the bride remain conscious that this closeness will temporarily subside as she approaches the wedding day and moves into her identity as wife. As Victoria intuitively felt, she needed to separate from her friends after the ritual to know that she could be without them after the wedding. This is not to say that a woman cannot have intimacy with other women once she marries. On the contrary, these relationships are essential to maintaining balance in her marriage. Rather, there may be a period where she needs to remove herself from the memories and symbolism they carry in order to establish her identity as wife on fresh ground. As Helen said three weeks before her wedding, "I've unquestionably pulled back from my girlfriends in the last five weeks, even the ones who are married. I've still been in contact but I haven't been calling out as much as I normally would. There's been a need to pull inward and remove myself from their world during this time."

Leaving the Nest: Separating from Mother

As the bride leaves her single life behind, she also loosens the strands that bind her to her mother. Of course, the crossing from daughter to wife does not mean that one ceases to be a daughter, but the importance of the daughter identity is diminished. A woman's age, the geographic distance between her and her mother, and the intensity of the particular mother-daughter relationship all help determine how difficult this separation will be. In some cases, mother and daughter will strengthen their bond through planning the wedding and sharing emotions during this exciting time; in other cases, the relationship remains unchanged. But in most cases, as the bride separates from her family of origin, the mother-daughter relationship will endure a significant change. This can be a difficult separation, because whether the relationship is intimate or estranged, an intensely strong bond exists.

The pain involved in the separation between mother and daughter around the wedding is poignantly depicted in the Greek myth of Persephone and Demeter. Persephone, simply referred to as Kore (meaning "maiden") in the beginning of the myth, is introduced while she is out gathering flowers with her friends. She is attracted to one particular flower, a beautiful narcissus, but when she reaches down to pick it, the ground splits open and she is dragged into an abyss by Hades, god of the underworld. Persephone struggles and screams for help from her father, but to no avail.

Demeter, Persephone's mother, hears her daughter's cries emanating from beneath the earth and frantically searches for her for nine days and nine nights. Finally she learns that her daughter has been kidnapped and forced to be Hades' bride. Demeter pleads for Zeus, father of the gods, to release Persephone. At first Zeus refuses, but eventually he succumbs to the mother's pleas and sends the messenger Hermes to recover Persephone. Persephone's despair turns to delight when Hermes informs her that he has come for her; however, before she leaves, Hades gives her some pomegranate seeds. By eating them, she unwittingly binds herself to spend a portion of the year in the underworld with her husband. The rest of the time she lives with her mother, Demeter, in the upper world.

This myth expresses the pain that may arise between mother and daughter when the young woman decides to marry. During the engagement a woman may feel, like Persephone, pulled between her mother and her fiancé. Suddenly, on the brink of a life-changing event, the beloved's arms may feel like Hades' underworld, a bit unknown, while the mother's arms feel familiar and comforting. Throughout her engagement she may feel as if she is teetering between comfort and mystery, old and new, mother and husband, daughter and wife. Carmen succinctly illustrated this split when she related her engagement story:

My fiancé proposed in front of my entire family at a Christmas party. He put the ring on my finger and my first response (and he still gets mad at me) was, "I don't know. Mom, what should I do?!" My mom said, "Just give him an answer, Carmen!" I said yes, but I was so shocked.

Her answer to the proposal came from the mouth of a little girl. She felt that she was on the brink of a large, life-altering decision and turned to her mother for the solution. Fortunately, unlike Demeter, who could not release her daughter, her mother pushed her little girl out of the nest and forced her to make the decision on her own. And in the months that followed, Carmen began to recognize the ways in which she was leaving her daughter role and assuming the role of wife: "I really feel like I am going to be taking my mom's place. I am taking on my mom's role but it feels like such a big role. I feel like the torch is being passed."

Perhaps of all the separations that occur during this transition, the one between mother and daughter is the most difficult. Even if a woman lost her mother early in life or has not spoken to her in many years, this primary relationship forms the blueprint for many of her decisions, thoughts, emotions, and actions. And if a woman is particularly close to her mother, she may need to keep reminding herself that this is a time of separation if she is to remove herself from her mother's strong embrace. For many women, the wedding may be the first time in their lives that they have been called to separate from their mother. In these cases, it is particularly important that the bride spend significant time exploring her thoughts and feelings about this relationship.

Whether the relationship is estranged or intimate, the energy of Mother may play a prominent role during the rites of separation. During this first phase of the rite of passage, when the bride feels as if she is dying or losing her familiar identity, she may long for a real or imagined mother, because this concept represents safety, comfort, and familiarity. Paulina shared:

About two months before my wedding I felt a longing to return home. I hadn't lived at home in several years so this longing didn't make sense to me. All I knew was that I wanted to be in my mother's presence as a single, unmarried daughter one last time. I wanted to be the kid and she could be the adult. It felt like my marriage was pushing me into a new phase of responsible adulthood and I wanted to drag my feet a little longer before stepping into those shoes.

The bride simultaneously longs for this dependent state and feels herself being pushed to grow beyond it. Needless to say, we do not often leave this state voluntarily, but just as babies are forced from their mother's womb at birth, adults are also shaken from the solidity of familiar ground when called to move into the next stage of growth. A woman cannot enter into a new identity and partnership if she is still clinging to old familiar ways.

The roots of love and attachment run deep for both mother and daughter. Today, although a woman may have separated geographically from her mother many years before the wedding and no longer considers herself "her mother's daughter," she still finds her mother's presence returning during the transition. Sophia, who had not lived at home in six years and had endured many painful periods of separation from her mother, was surprised by her mother's presence in her inner life:

My mother loomed large in my pre-wedding life. This surprised me because I had separated from her geographically many years earlier and I felt that I had become an adult in my own right. But my mother is a powerful woman, and in retrospect I understand that before I married I had to reconcile her influence on my psychological life and the effect that my childhood relationship with her would have on my upcoming marriage. My engagement initiated a process that is still in motion: finding who I am apart from who she believes I am and coming "into my own" as a woman.

When the bond between mother and daughter is either too tight or too loose, the separation is quite confusing. If the boundary between them has not been clearly drawn, a bride may carry over this unhealthy pattern into her relationship with her fiancé, resulting in a fear of suffocation on her part. On the other hand, if her mother is a cold, controlling woman, she may feel dumbfounded at the prospect of assuming the role of wife. She has had little role-modeling of a nurturing, warm woman and may feel as if she is floundering in the assumption that she should know how to carry this role. In this case, her fears of abandonment will come to the surface. Most mother-daughter relationships, carrying strains of both elements, cause women to stumble through this phase of initiation. As Diana, who married in her mid-thirties, remarked, "What it felt like was that I collapsed and my mother came and lived in my skin. . . . I couldn't find who I was in the midst of all this."

The consequences for refusing this separation are profound, and it is the responsibility of both mother and daughter to ensure that the break occurs. Wallerstein and Blakeslee emphasize that one of the foundations of a healthy marriage is for the bride and groom to separate emotionally from their families and elevate their spouse to top priority. Referring to the bride's journey, they write: "Separation is particularly tricky for women because the ties between mother and daughter, made up of powerful strands of compassion, love, and sometimes guilt, are so powerful. . . . Marriage may be particularly hard for the daughter whose mother is lonely and unhappy or is caring for an ill sibling or spouse" (55).

What is painful for the bride may be equally painful for the mother. Sensing this grief, some brides nuzzle closer to their mothers during the engagement, using the planning to strengthen the bond *and* as a way to distract themselves from their feelings of loss. Just as the unconscious resistance to the proposal is transferred onto the ring, the unconscious emotional undercurrents of loss and grief are transferred onto the planning. Because control is often an attempt to defend against loss, mothers may gallop onto the scene with an urgent need to take charge of the details of the planning. Kelsey noticed that her single mother, who had "broken down a few times when it would hit her that I was leaving," charged full force into attending to the most minute details in the days prior to the event. Kelsey remembered:

All of her perfectionism came out. She had people coming to clean the windows that day. She made her own stress—I didn't care if the windows were clean! She had all these expectations and Thursday was her last shot to do everything. We had a huge argument where she tore into me, both of us yelling at the top of our lungs. I said, "What's your problem? You're so distant from me. You've never done this before." On some level I knew that she was freaking out about me getting married and losing me. But she was so wound up in the planning and excitement that it didn't hit her until after the wedding. Then she wrote me a letter and apologized, telling me she had freaked out because of the loss.

Kelsey and her mother had grown very close just prior to the wedding. Kelsey, like several other brides, had felt drawn to move home before her wedding, ostensibly to facilitate the planning but also to live together as mother and daughter one last time and solidify their bond:

My wedding was in southern California and I was living in northern California, so a month and a half before the wedding I came down and lived with my mom. It was incredible. I felt so good with my mom. It was wonderful to have that time together to reconnect. But it was hard for her when I left.

In themselves, these ways of connecting do not pose a serious threat. However, both mother and daughter need to realize that this phase is coming to an end and that after the wedding the bride's allegiance will need to shift to her husband. It is important to bring the unconscious emotional impulse for these reunions to the surface so that mother and daughter can consciously grieve together and prepare the bride for her new role.

No Longer Number One: Separating from Father

Bonds between a bride and her father can be equally tight and the change in this relationship also needs to be grieved. Father, like Mother, appears in both his symbolic and literal forms. Symbolically, the father embodies the masculine principle, which cuts ties with sharpness and precision. This principle is represented in the myth of Persephone when Zeus, the father, initially refuses to rescue his daughter from the underworld. It is also represented in the wedding when the father "gives away" his daughter.

The realization of this inevitable giving away needs to begin long before the wedding day. A bride who does not begin to loosen the ties to her father until after she weds only exacerbates the difficulty she may have of transferring her priorities onto her husband. Kelsey realized during her engagement that she needed to talk to her dad about the loss she was feeling. She and her father had always enjoyed a very close relationship and she was afraid that she would "lose it emotionally" on her wedding day around the symbolic gestures that symbolized "leaving him." (She had not actually lived with him in many years, but she still felt as if she were leaving him.) Six months before her wedding, she said:

There are certain images that make me almost break down when I think of them. One is when we walk down the aisle and my dad lets go of my hand, then sits behind me as I walk up to the altar. I will feel the loss in that act. I mean, that's it, that's the separation. Or even dancing with my dad: There's a song that my dad and I are probably going to dance to and whenever I put it on, I start crying.

In contemplating these images, she decided she needed to talk to her father before the wedding day. The two spent a few hours talking about their relationship and how it would change with her marriage. Her father shared that it was hard for him that she was changing her last name, that the act felt symbolic of her transference of loyalties from father to husband. As much as he loved her fiancé and supported her marriage, he still felt the sadness at losing his little girl. Kelsey said: "We had a good cry together, which was very bonding and releasing." Kelsey felt much clearer after their conversation, as if she could move into her new role without carrying the burden of both her and her father's sadness within her.

Where the mother may use control to defend against loss, the father may focus on economic matters as a way to deflect his sorrow at losing his little girl. (This is also a form of control.) When the bridegroom offers his opinions about the finer points of the wedding plans, he may be sidelined by the booming voice of a father who knows best and is, after all, paying for the affair. Frances and Tom still have "sour feelings" about the events that took place between them and Frances's father, Ken, before their wedding:

Tom had clear ideas about us leaving the reception in a limousine. My dad had previously agreed to pay for the limousine but at the last moment rescinded his agreement on the account that it was "a frivolous expense." Tom was angry that my dad made this decision without asking us, and more angry that the entire interaction occurred with me as the liaison. Tensions escalated over what should have been a minor issue until my dad and I had a full blown, screaming battle. He even threatened that he would not attend the wedding. I left the house and did not return until the middle of the night. The argument was smoothed over but something within my relationship with my dad was ruptured. Those arguments before the wedding caused irreparable damage between my father and me. Neither of us understood what happened.

Instead of Ken acknowledging his sadness, he redirected his uncomfortable feelings onto a trivial issue, making Tom the target of his pent-up energy and causing his daughter a lot of pain.

The preexisting tensions between father and bridegroom can become particularly acute during this period. Often, the father simultaneously harbors resentment toward the man who is "stealing" his daughter while agreeing to the union and pushing his girl out the door. This is not an easy task, and although he may consent, he may also assert his dominance in the last months of this phase of his fatherhood. Recognizing and consciously grieving the loss could alleviate much conflict and aggression. As we see with Frances and her father, when loss is ignored, it creeps in through the back door and makes itself known in unpleasant ways.

The wedding, as a microcosm of life, not only emphasizes the characters who are active in the bride's life but also illuminates those who are missing. Some brides have suffered the loss of one or both parents due to emotional distance, divorce, or death. Other brides mourn the absence of a particularly close grandparent who was unable to witness her wedding. The wedding can also bring into stark relief the losses that the bride may have suffered many years earlier: an absent father, a mother who skipped town, an estranged sibling. Few people these days can claim a *Leave It to Beaver*-type household, yet the expectation of an intact and congenial family is still there. While some women may grieve the separation from a warm, supportive father, for example, other women may grieve the ways in which her father failed her, or even the complete absence of a father in her life. It is important to allow ourselves to consciously grieve these absences. If we don't, they will often make themselves known on the wedding day. As Diana said:

My father was like a missing prop at my wedding. He passed away when I was eighteen, twenty years before I got married, so my relationship with him is a total mystery to me. On my wedding day, I think there was some conscious effort not to look at all that wasn't there—the family that wasn't there, the love that was missing. I tried very hard to keep all the pain at bay. The result was that I wasn't present at all, my energy so consumed by keeping out the emotions, the losses, and the absences that seemed too painful to feel.

Often the issues around one's father are brought to the fore when it comes time to decide who is going to walk the bride down the aisle. Carmen was having a traditional wedding and so agreed to have her father walk her down. She said it felt like more of a concession to him than something that she truly wanted:

I have to say that it feels strange. I have threatened that if he didn't pay for this wedding then he couldn't walk me down the aisle. I feel like I am allowing him to play

*his role as "father of the bride" because he's paying for
the wedding. But I feel that there have been other people
more influential in my upbringing. If I want to show
symbolically who is "giving me away" it would be my
mom. To me that would be more meaningful and
emotional than my dad.*

*This wedding is a gift to me to replace something
that my father could never give. The only way he can
show his love is through money. So now, finally, it's my
way of saying, "Show me how much you love me, Dad."
But the truth is that I want something that he can never
give me. If somebody told me, "If you gave up this
wedding you could have your dad's love," I would give it
all up for that. But that's not an option, so I might as
well take what I can get. It's very painful and I think it
was the wedding that really brought it into focus.*

Lydia had a particularly powerful separation from her
father on her wedding day. Although she has been married
for sixteen years and has three children, she still looks back
on the experience with her father with strong emotion. She
wrote, "I have been thinking about ways my husband and I
can support our children through this important rite of passage. They should not have to go through it alone, left to
pick up the pieces of unacknowledged transition many years
later, as I have." She described the scene at her wedding and
the unresolved emotions about the relationship with her
father:

*It is the relationship with my father that stands out most
when I think back on my wedding day. I see him hanging
around me, or onto me, as if he didn't quite know how
to say goodbye. While my mother was bustling about in a
matter-of-fact mode, my father seemed lost. He wandered
around with a hazy look on his face, not quite sure where*

to be or what to say. I remember that he wanted to talk to me and that I was not in the mood. I had all these "details" that I had to take care of. Of course, knowing what I know now, I see many of those details as a convenient shield against the emotions that threatened to pour down my face. I also did not know how to say goodbye. I didn't even know that I was supposed to say goodbye!

One moment in my wedding day brings tears to my eyes when I think about it. My father gave me a necklace as a symbolic gesture of his love (and probably, in some way, a goodbye). Then, right before we were to walk down the aisle, he wanted to get mushy ("mushy" is how it felt to me at the time). But I did not want to be crying as I walked down the aisle and I was angry at him for being sentimental at the wrong time. So I turned away. I shut him out because I was in no way prepared for the emotions a conversation such as that would have elicited. I know I must have hurt his feelings. I know I lost a precious opportunity. I would have liked him to approach me that morning or the day before. I wonder if some part of him purposely chose a time that we could not fully express our emotions. To fully recognize and express the largeness of this moment would have been too hard for him as well.

I have no idea if he has any leftover feelings about that day. I'd like to talk with him about it. The wedding changed our relationship in many ways, ways that I was not even conscious of until now. It's painful to think about it. I'm realizing that I did lose my father that day. It must have been so hard for him and I was not sensitive to it at all. But how could I have been? I had no idea what was happening. In hindsight, I can only imagine what it must have felt like to be "replaced." I bet it didn't feel very good. Lately I have been aware that a subtle shift occurred after my wedding day in the way he relates to me. I believe now that it has to do with him not knowing how he fits into my life anymore. He was always very good at giving advice and telling me what to do. I obviously don't need that anymore (and probably never did to the degree he thought!), but I need to talk to him and let him know what it is that I do need from him. I think it would really help us both.

Her story is a clear message to brides, encouraging them to address the changes in their relationships before the wedding. It is also a message to fathers to begin to recognize their changing role in their daughter's life. Whatever the particular circumstances surrounding the bride's relationship with her father, if the loss is recognized, it can funnel into its appropriate form of expression. Otherwise, the bride is left a tangled mass of confusion, trying to repair the impossible or denying the child's tears that beg to be released.

Loss of Identity: Separating from the Identity as a Single Woman

In the final phases of the separation process, the bride endures the most unnerving loss of all: the loss of the identity she has carried until this moment in her life. If a woman feels like she is dying in the months before her wedding, that is because she is experiencing the sacrifice of an aspect of herself. She has separated from her friends, sisters, mother, and father; now, stripped down to the core of her being, she prepares for the final layer of loss. While brides are usually filled with excitement as the wedding day nears, the joy can be tempered by feelings of loss and confusion around the transformation of identity. As Helen shared:

I feel like I'm jumping off a cliff and wondering when I start walking on the bottom who I'm going to become. It feels like such a transformation. I've been acting strange, much more introverted, quiet. It's like I can't feel myself and I can't feel my love for my fiancé. I said to him the other day, "I just want you to know that I'm not normally who I've been in the last month and a half."

Helen is in the midst of her transformation from one identity and way of life to another. She is *not* who she normally is, which is exactly appropriate for this stage of her process. Helen also had a strong sense that she was leaving a way of life that worked as a single woman but that would no longer correspond to the commitment she was making:

I feel like I'm dying to a whole way of life. I've had a certain way of relating to men that was easy to do when I was single, but as a married person it's not okay. When I was in sales, flirtation was part of it. It feels threatening to think about losing that, and yet I know that I will. My upcoming marriage is the most important thing in my life. I will do anything to protect it. So if that means changing how I relate to 50 percent of the people out there, that's what I will do. That's what I'm doing. But it's a pretty big transition, changing a whole way of being in the world.

Helen's sense of leaving a way of life had external elements. Shortly before her wedding, she said:

I've had a strong desire to go through my closet and throw out half my stuff and literally change my identity!

Since I've moved into his apartment I've had a strong sense of wanting to redo everything. I want to redecorate and have a new everything. It definitely feels symbolic of this change of identity. I can feel myself shedding many aspects of the life I have led up to this time, my life as an unmarried person.

For the transformation to be complete, the woman must let go of her current identity. Women who refused to make this transition suffered the consequences in their first year of marriage. Samantha, now divorced, shares that her first thought when her husband proposed was, "Oh my god, I can never have sex with anyone else again." She agreed to marry him with the hope that marriage would "cure" her so she wouldn't be attracted to other men, but looking back she realizes that she was unable to let go of the lifestyle of a single woman. Six months after the wedding, she began an affair that ultimately ended her marriage.

The change of identity and loss of maidenhood are underlined by the loss of one's *maiden* name. As with the ring, feminists have criticized the change of name for its roots in patriarchal practices of female subordination. Many women in recent years have decided to retain their maiden name as a statement of independence and equality. While this impulse is certainly understandable, it overlooks the symbolic resonance and bypasses one of this culture's few rituals for transformation. To change one's last name and take on the name of one's spouse assumes an element of surrender. It also concretely acknowledges that a change of identity has occurred. Bruce Lincoln, in *Emerging from the Chrysalis*, relates this to indigenous practice: "The girl's proper name is bestowed on her only after she has been initiated, become an adult, lost her maiden status. Such a change of name is a regular feature in the initiatory rites of innumerable people as a mark of the initiand's total transformation" (79).

For women who marry later in life or who feel that they have surrendered enough of themselves during this process, or in other areas of their lives, the change may feel intolerable. As Diana said:

It was very important for me to keep my last name. I didn't associate it with anything political or social; it was a way of hanging on to myself, to my identity. I didn't want to create a new identity as his wife in such an explicit way. It would have pushed me over the edge into unreality if I went from Diana Hansen to Diana Lutz. I felt like I surrendered so much of my identity in this process that to do that would have felt like I was bordering on having no identity base at all. I had had my name for thirty-eight years and I saw no reason to give that up too.

On the other hand, for women who marry in their late teens or early twenties when their identity is still in the process of forming, the change may feel less distinct. Brenda married at twenty-one and said:

Of course I took his last name. I didn't even think about it. I was so young when I married and had not yet formed a definite identity. I didn't know what my calling would be and there was a way in which I didn't know who I was. I wanted to shed my name and take on his.

Isabel felt it was important to retain her maiden name because it represented her cultural identity. Yet she also wanted to join with her husband and assume his name. She was clear from the beginning that she would hyphenate:

I'm Isabel Garcia-McGowen. I'm very proud of who I am,
which is a Mexican-American woman. I wasn't ready to
lose my identity by dropping the Garcia because that is
part of who I am. Had his name been Marcus Gonzales I
would have changed my name. For me it was essential to
maintain my connection to my heritage.

Sara and Victoria surprised themselves with the imme-
diacy with which they were willing to change their last name.
Victoria never thought she would change her last name, a
feeling enforced by growing up with a mother who retained
her maiden name. When her best friend married and
changed her last name, Victoria was surprised. But the surprise ended when she met her fiancé and felt overwhelmingly
clear that she wanted to assume his name. From nearly the
moment they met, she never wavered on her decision. She
wanted to merge with him and become one family unit, and
she did not equate her decision with a loss of her individual
identity or independence as a woman. Sara, on the other
hand, vacillated on her decision throughout her engagement:

As a teenager and throughout college, I had prided myself
on my independence and equality as a woman and
silently chided women who succumbed to the patriarchal
practice of changing one's last name. But when I met my
husband, the thought of having two separate names no
longer appealed to me. I wanted to unite with him, to be
one family with one last name.

At various moments throughout the engagement I
would go back on my decision. The loss of my maiden
name felt symbolic of the loss of my identity as a single
woman and a degree of independence. Sometimes I felt
like my individuality was being sucked into the whirlpool
of our love and my name, the name that I had written
on thousands of papers, signed on checks, the name

printed on every legal document from my birth certificate to my passport, was the raft that held me afloat. In the end, my visceral longing overrode both my fears and my mind's attempts at intellectual persuasion. In the depths of my soul, I wanted to become Sara Erikson.

The enormity of the name change is not to be underestimated. Women of all ages and from all walks of life struggled with the decision. Jade, who began dating her husband when she was eighteen, had always thought she would change her last name. But at twenty-six, and three months after her wedding, she found herself resisting:

I'm still battling whether to change my last name. I had always romanticized changing my name, of course I would! But as I grew up and created an identity aside from ours, I thought, "No, that's not just the obvious conclusion." I think we are going to follow the Mexican tradition where the children's middle name will be my maiden name and I will hyphenate. I really like his last name but I don't think that I'm willing to give up my last name, nor should I. It feels like possession, ownership. Part of our vows to each other a long time ago was that there was no possession or ownership and that we would love each other until that was no longer working. I'm feeling pressured to change my last name by banks and establishments. But it feels like it's giving up a part of my identity, and I ask myself, why aren't men asked to give up something too? I'm still coming to terms with that. It's really confusing. It's something as small as changing names but it feels really huge.

As with the proposal and the ring, the bride may resist what feels like another abduction. Like her mother, she may consume herself with the "doing" aspects of this time to avoid being pulled into a whirlpool of loss. Like her father, she may begin to view her beloved bridegroom as an unattractive captor and turn from him with a degree of horror. As Jade said of her husband: "Since the wedding I've been more intolerant of the same things he's always done. Sometimes I've even been slightly repulsed by him, which is so strange because I've been consistently attracted to him for eight years!" At these times it is reassuring to recall that the oracle in Psyche's story prophesied that Psyche would marry Death and instead she found herself betrothed to the god of love. Robert Johnson noted: "The oracle was right; a man is death to a woman in an archetypal sense. When a man sees an anguished look on his partner's face, this is a time to be gentle and cautious; it may be that she is just waking up to the fact that she is dying a little as maiden" (17).

Regardless of where the bride falls on her last name decision, at some point it is crucial that she grieve the loss of singlehood that the maiden name represents. The length and intensity of this grief differ for everyone. For Victoria the grief appeared sporadically in brief moments over a period of several months; for Helen it slayed her for two weeks and then reappeared after the wedding for a few days. Although we are using words like "death" and "sacrifice," the grieving does not need to be a heavy, drawn-out process. In fact, the more thoroughly we can allow ourselves to feel the grief whenever it surfaces, the more quickly it will pass. The psychological adage "What we resist, persists," holds especially true for the wedding. The bride has so many emotions and experiences to contend with that it would be most helpful for her to allow each one its full expression when it arises. So when the option of grieving loss presents itself before the actual loss occurs, the opportunity should be seized. Isabel shared her experience:

I got so emotional the night before my wedding. Our friend who married us was at the table and she said,

"Isabel, why are you crying?" and I said, "I have no idea." It was an overwhelming sense of mourning that I was no longer a maiden, but I didn't know that until years later. I think the reason that I was able to feel that level of mourning was that I didn't put a lot of energy into the wedding planning. I planned it in a week! And that was it for my grieving. After that it didn't come up again. Even though I wasn't aware of what I was feeling I allowed myself to feel it. I really cried. I let it out that whole night. It was very cleansing and therapeutic. And that was it for my mourning. I felt light on my wedding day and it felt fantastic to be married.

In whatever manner, the bride must unfasten the ropes that tether her to an old way of life. This can be a painful process, but it can also be a liberating one. Many of the brides felt relieved when they finally faced the pain around the losses and took the necessary action that allowed it to pass through. Sometimes that action was having a conversation with the person involved—mother, father, girlfriend. Sometimes a ritual was needed to let go of an aspect of the single identity. Helen felt the need for closure around her last significant relationship before she met her fiancé. She had no desire to talk to the ex-beau but she felt that through writing about any lingering feelings and creating a closing ritual with some photographs she would open the space that the relationship was occupying internally. Kathryn knew that her absent father would bring pain on her wedding day and she wanted to work through some of those feelings beforehand. She spent a day writing in her journal and allowed herself to feel another layer of the loss she had always felt around their relationship. And Sara, knowing that her role as caretaker for her single mother would be altered after her wedding, decided she wanted to talk with her mother about the impending change. After two conversations the air was clear and they both felt more ready to accept the changes. As the bride lets go of her singlehood identity, she prepares an internal space where her new identity as wife will eventually bloom.

Questions to Contemplate

🐚 Think about your engagement. Did your fiancé propose to you formally? If so, how did you feel when he proposed? If not, how did you feel when the two of you decided to get married? Did your proposal meet your expectations?

🐚 How do you feel about your engagement ring? What are some of the thoughts you have when you see it on your finger?

🐚 How does it feel to be engaged?

🐚 Have you noticed any changes in your relationships with your girlfriends since you've been engaged? What kinds of thoughts have you had about your childhood, adolescence, and time as a single woman? Have you felt more or less drawn to spend time with your girlfriends since your engagement?

🐚 Spend some time thinking about your relationship with your father. Have you noticed any significant changes in the relationship in the last few months? If you are close to your father, how do you feel about symbolically "leaving" him when you marry, even if you physically left him years ago? Have you discussed any of these feelings with him? If you do not have a close relationship with your father, or if he has passed away, what feelings have arisen with regard to him lately?

🐚 Explore the feelings that have arisen with regard to your mother recently. What does your mother symbolize to you? Do you feel that your relationship will be altered by the marriage? In what ways do you feel that you are leaving your primary identity as daughter as you prepare to step into the role of wife?

❦ During the engagement you may feel pulled between your mother and your fiancé. Explore how this pattern is playing itself out in your life. How does your mother feel about your fiancé? Have you been pulled to return to your mother's house at any point in the engagement?

❦ Often, when we are unaware of the emotions in our lives, they make themselves known through our bodies. Have you noticed any physical changes since the engagement? Changes in eating habits? Sleeping patterns? Exercise routine? After exploring any changes, take some time to consider what messages are veiled in the language of your body.

❦ Do you plan to change your last name? What thoughts and feelings have contributed to this decision? If you are planning to change your name, practice writing your married signature as a way of taking the concept of the name change out of your head and bringing it into your body. How does it feel to write your new name? How does it feel to let go of your maiden name? If you have chosen to keep your maiden name, what feelings do you have about this decision?

Chapter Three

The Quest for Perfection

I didn't want a normal wedding. In fact, I didn't want a wedding at all. But one thing led to another and before I knew it we were having a pretty traditional affair with two hundred and forty people. All of a sudden I was in a wedding frenzy. I was spending hours thinking about what kind of dress I was going to wear. It shocked me when I realized that I had gotten into the bride mode. And even more shocking was the lengths I was willing to go to be the *perfect bride* for this day. I felt possessed by this wedding planning, the perfectionism of it all.

—Vivian

I was spending money hand over fist to make everything look so perfect. I just depended on what I had learned from my mother and the life I had grown up in because I knew that it was societally correct and would impress everybody. You know, the engraved invitations and everything in silk and taffeta, the handwritten menus, the right band, the right champagne. It wasn't me. After the wedding I felt an immense sense of self-betrayal because the wedding was not an expression of us but an empty event where everything looked perfect.

—Diana

All of my fears about relationships seem to have intensified as the wedding approaches: will he leave me? Will I leave him? Will he cheat on me? Will he die? Right now we are so happy together, but I see so many couples where the love has gone out of their marriage and it scares me. It scares me because we don't have many role-models for lifelong, loving relationships.

—Cora

The "Perfect" Defense

If there is one word that falls from a bride's lips more often than any other during her engagement, it is "perfect": "I just found the *perfect* dress!" "We finally found our location; it's *perfect*." "He proposed to me on the bridge overlooking the bay—it was *perfect*!" When a bride is consumed by the energy of her wedding, she often finds that the expectation of perfection rears its head with fierce insistence and seeps into every crevice of the event. Everything around the wedding in our culture points to perfection. Magazines and bridal shows have no qualms about encouraging the bride to create a perfect day. Even women who never thought they would succumb to the popular wedding images and messages surprised themselves with their drive toward perfection. Vivian said:

I didn't want a normal wedding. In fact, I didn't want a wedding at all. But one thing led to another and before I knew it we were having a pretty traditional affair with two hundred and forty people. All of a sudden I was in a wedding frenzy. I was spending hours thinking about what kind of dress I was going to wear. It shocked me when I realized that I had gotten into the bride mode. And even more shocking was the lengths I was willing to go to be the "perfect bride" for this day. I am the most un-vain person I know but three days before the wedding my sister convinced me to get my upper lip waxed. I had never had anything waxed in my life and all of a sudden this became very important and I was thinking, "Oh thank god! I almost had a mustache walking down the aisle—angel of mercy!" I felt possessed by this wedding planning, the perfectionism of it all.

Many brides used the word "possessed" to describe the perfectionistic energy that surrounded the wedding planning. Diana remembered the moment this energy came over her:

I was sitting on the bed with my legs crossed, reading bridal magazines, which was very uncharacteristic of me, and I felt like this spirit entered my body and took control. It was like being possessed. And whatever that energy was, it was what drove me through all the plans, all the guest lists. It piloted me through to the end of the wedding day.

Vivian was bewildered by the feeling. Diana felt "devoured" by it. How can we understand this energy that seems to prey on the most unsuspecting brides? Part of it stems from the media messages we receive: Not only is the wedding to be a purely joyous day but it must also be flawless. It is nearly impossible to live in our culture without absorbing this message. Yet the message is merely a magnification of the perfectionism that fuels every sector of our culture.

Perfectionism's function is to keep people busy and cut off from their authentic emotional experience. When the mind is occupied and moving at a frenetic pace, there is little room left for feelings. Perfectionism keeps us externally focused, perennially attempting to achieve what our culture deems ideal, perennially walled off from the mysterious churnings of our internal lives. We live in a culture where we are trying to outrun the mystery of life. Because Westerners feel tremendous anxiety when they simply sit still, we will go to great lengths to organize our lives so that all available time slots are occupied by meetings and activities. We believe that if we consume ourselves with acts of doing, we can avoid sitting with the contents of our being. Doing, achieving, and the pursuit of perfection are sibling stitches in the fabric of this culture, and they weave themselves particularly tightly around the bride.

As a product of this culture, the bride may feel that if she were to stop and sit still for a moment she would be overcome by torrents of emotion, including loss, fear, and loneliness. Since she has had few lessons in life on how to manage these feelings, she may feel that if she stops for a moment they will come crashing down upon her. The feelings can be temporarily kept at bay through keeping busy. In this vein, the bride dives into the schedules, lists, and deadlines that form the blueprint of her wedding. If she fills her days with tasks and chores, she leaves no empty space for the deeper springs of life to bubble to the surface of her experience. For it is in the emptiness, the quiet moments in the day when we sit beside a tree or stare into the blankness of the sky, that the underside of life is allowed to tiptoe to the edge of our conscious minds.

There is no better way to keep oneself busy than through the pursuit of perfection, and when this drive seizes a bride, she becomes consumed by a force greater than herself. Because Western weddings are characterized by the completion of task after tiny task, her perfectionism is often let loose from the moment a woman becomes engaged. Opening any bridal magazine, one will find pages of "helpful hints," which often include detailed worksheets on such subjects as: "Who's in charge of what on our wedding day?" or "Reception checklist" or "Photography checklist."

When a bride focuses on perfection she allows herself the illusion of control. But most likely she feels quite out of control, as if she is helplessly tumbling inside a giant wave. To avoid experiencing a loss of control, she may cling to these wedding tasks, which beckon her perfectionistic tendencies into the light. Tasks are definite; they can be completed and checked off a list, and they provide a sort of life raft the bride can cling to. Emotions are amorphous and confusing, and if she doesn't have a context in which to view them during times of psychological transition, they are particularly frightening. It is never pleasant to feel out of control, and less so if she doesn't understand what is happening. She may feel that if she exerts control and maintains order in the external world, her inner world will follow suit. Unfortunately, the tender soul generally balks in the face of forcefully imposed standards. Perhaps if the bride were to surrender to the swirling of the wave, terrifying as it is, she would eventually be spit onto shore.

Perfectionism is, primarily, a need to control. And control is a mask, or protection, against feeling difficult emotions. Any time we find ourselves trying to control a situation, it is because we are unconsciously trying to defend against feeling our grief, fear, helplessness, or loneliness. We control, defend, and become perfectionistic when we are unwilling to let go and surrender. This drive to perfectionism, although understandable, does not serve the bride positively. It keeps her divorced from her inner realms, from the emotions that need to be expressed and processed during this time. The problem, or blessing, with perfectionism is that it cannot maintain its grip forever. Eventually, usually after the wedding, the porcelain mask that has propelled the bride through her engagement will crumble. Diana talked about the consequences of this pattern:

I wouldn't surrender anything. I wouldn't let go of control. I wouldn't face my fears. I wouldn't let people love me. I wouldn't feel anything. I wouldn't feel that my father wasn't there and that my family was broken up. I wouldn't feel all the loss and sacrifice I had been experiencing. I was unwilling to notice any loss or death prior to the event even though it was sucking everything out of me. Once the wedding passed, all of that came back on me. Every time I opened my eyes, I felt like I was dying. I spent my first months of marriage in a deep depression because of everything I refused to feel before the wedding.

The deaths and losses that begged to be acknowledged before the wedding were silenced beneath the perfectionistic drive that possessed Diana. If she had known that she was allowed and supposed to feel uncomfortable feelings during this time, she would have been able to approach her wedding day with a great deal more serenity. There are three main emotions the bride faces: grief, fear, and loneliness. As we have already seen in chapter three, *grief* surfaces in response to the separation process. Deaths of any nature necessitate grief, and as the bride separates and psychologically dies to the identity she has always known, she will allow herself to mourn these changes. But two other difficult emotions also accompany brides through the engagement: the *fear* of marriage and the *loneliness* of transition.

To marry these days is an act of faith. Most brides are acutely aware of the high divorce rate in this country and many of us come from "broken" homes ourselves. We are aware that when we marry we surrender ourselves to love, and with this surrender comes the possibility of losing this love to either divorce, deflation of the love, or death. The awareness of these possibilities surfaces as a fear of the commitment of marriage. Brides ask themselves: What if I lose my husband? What if he leaves me? What if he falls out of love with me? What if I fall out of love with him? What if I lose myself in the marriage, sacrifice too much of myself for the marriage? Again, brides feel that they cannot speak these queries aloud, for whenever they mention them they are met with, "Are you having second thoughts about getting married?" Conscious questioning of legitimate issues should not be equated with doubt. On the contrary, it is usually when brides feel secure in their love and commitment that they can venture to ask these difficult questions. And why shouldn't they ask? How many of us know more than a handful of couples who are living examples of loving, vital marriages? It is essential that brides are encouraged to ask the questions and feel the fears that arise through the asking.

Emily was visited by a host of prewedding fears five months before her wedding. Psychologically astute, she said that her fears vacillated between the two traditional fears that play themselves out in intimate relationships: the fear of her fiancé leaving her for someone else or abandoning her in some other way and the fear of her loss of freedom and loss of self. She had several dreams that began with "Mark is not going to marry me" and other dreams that depicted the other end of the spectrum, where she felt suffocated by him. She wrote in her journal:

Spending the rest of our lives together—my God. Mark looks at me across the table and says, "I feel so happy knowing that we will grow old together," and depending on my state of fear or excitement, that sentence either terrifies me or thrills me.

Emily spent a lot of time writing in her journal about these fears. Whenever she met a couple who had been married several years and still seemed to enjoy each other, she quizzed them about what made their marriage work. By the time she met her fiancé at the altar her fears were significantly reduced.

Cora was also in touch with her prewedding fears. Eight months before her wedding, she said:

All of my fears about relationships seem to have intensified as the wedding approaches: Will he leave me? Will I leave him? Will he cheat on me? Will he die? Right now we are so happy together, but I see so many couples

*where the love has gone out of their marriage and it
scares me. It scares me because we don't have many role
models for lifelong, loving relationships. When the love
goes out of the marriage, people give up. That's when the
affairs happen. I know coworkers who are in their forties
and having affairs. I want them to give me some hope
and they say, "Oh, you're still young, and you're still in
love. You'll understand," implying that as time goes by I,
too, will want to have an affair. I say to them, "I don't
want to understand that!" There has to be some hope
that it is possible to sustain a healthy, loving relationship.*

Kirsten, another young woman whose wedding was fast
approaching, had these fears about making a lifetime
commitment:

*I fear my fiancé will die. Actually, before I met Dan I
was the type of person that was afraid that the man I
married would cheat on me. My parents divorced when I
was very young and my dad had had an affair, so that's
what was role-modeled for me. But after five years of
being with Dan, I trust him completely. I don't have the
same fear I had before, so now there's the issue that I
don't have control over: What if he gets into an accident
and dies? I would be devastated. I honestly believe that
there is no one else like him. We completely accept and
love each other deeply. To lose someone that you love so
much, it's such a devastatingly painful loss.*

As with the grief of the separation process, it is important to allow these fears sufficient room to breathe. We may
not immediately find the answers to our concerns about
long-term marriages, but at least we can allow ourselves the
space to ask the questions. When we are about to step into
something unknown, it is highly likely that we will feel some
fear. If nothing else, the magnitude of the marriage

commitment will encourage every embedded fear to come out from the crannies of our psyches so that they can be addressed and, ultimately, healed. If we try to deny the existence of the fears, the possibility of healing them becomes more remote.

The grief and fear that surface during the engagement are intensified by the loneliness inherent to all transitions. The leap from one stage of life to another must be done alone. People can help guide the initiate along the way, offering words of wisdom and comfort, but the final transformation of identity occurs within the initiate's body. For example, when a woman is giving birth, people can offer support and attempt to ease the pain, but no one can have the baby for her. When a man reaches forty, he can alleviate some of his anxiety about the transition through discussions with other men, but no one can turn forty for him. All crossings, from birth through death, are made alone. It is part of the loneliness of being human.

When a bride feels *alone* during her engagement, it is because she is severed from the essential community of women that can assist her with many aspects of this crossing. But when she experiences *loneliness,* she knows that the deeper layers of this transformation are occurring and no one, not her fiancé, best friend, or mother, can make the transformation for her. Clare described the loneliness in her journal one week before her wedding:

I talked to Shawn this morning about how lonely I feel, like I am a child on the precipice of a magnificent leap and I am standing on the cliff alone, no one to guide me to the edge, no one to lend wisdom in the final leap, no one to whisper from the crevices as I fall, no one to meet me on the ground below. Yes, it is exciting, but it also scary in so many ways. No one can do this with me, not even him. It is lonely, and there is nothing anyone can do about it.

Loneliness is a difficult emotion to feel. We will do almost anything to avoid feeling the loneliness when it arises. The bride does not have to look far to deflect the feeling through an act of doing, but it is precisely at that moment, the moment when she reaches for the phone to call one more florist or picks up her wedding notebook to look over her checklists, that she should stop and ask herself what she truly needs. The florists and the checklists are temporary distractions. They siphon off the superficial layer of the loneliness, fear, or grief but do nothing to soothe the deeper waves. Only the bride can know what kind of "solo vision quest" she needs in order to make this transition. It may be something as simple as taking ten minutes a day just to *be*, time in which she allows whatever emotions are simmering within to surface.

A Mythological and Spiritual View

How else can we understand the perfectionism that so often consumes brides? Does it have any healthy functions in the wedding journey? As we have seen, and perhaps you have noticed within yourself, the over-focus on perfection can create a frenzied bride out of an otherwise sane and rational woman. But, if understood and channeled consciously, it can also serve a positive purpose. Its presence around the wedding can be understood through both a mythological and a spiritual lens.

The quest for perfection is actually a misguided attempt to follow a mythological pattern that calls for order in the face of a great challenge. Looking to Psyche's story, a wedding truth is revealed: Her first task is to sort an enormous pile of different kinds of seeds into their appropriate categories. She is required to "make form and order prevail." Is it possible that the checklists in bridal magazines are unwittingly attempting to facilitate this process? The bride's external world certainly can resemble a pile of different seeds that need to be sorted, and brides have found that the more organized they were externally, the more time and space they had to focus on their emotional world. Brides can derive real pleasure from making "form and order prevail" from the endless lists of things to do. As Anna said of her time as bride:

I wholeheartedly took on the business of being a bride-to-be. I wanted perfection for us on this special day. I had one of those brown accordion files where I kept every last detail organized: Our wedding site, the cake, my dress, flowers, photography, the ceremony, honeymoon, and bridal registry all had a separate file in my accordion. It began to billow and bulge as I filled each slot with information, receipts, and ideas.

Although Anna used the word *perfection*, and to some degree this was her goal, she was also able to funnel the perfection energy into the files of her accordion, and then leave it there while she spent time focusing on her inner world. She did not feel consumed with the perfection energy, but rather utilized it to help her create a beautiful day. Problems arise when, instead of the bride being in command of the energy, the energy takes charge of the bride. This is what created the sense of being "possessed by a demonic energy" that Diana spoke about. Her focus on the wedding ceased to be about creating a beautiful day as an expression of her and her fiancé's love, but became about fulfilling an externally imposed expectation for what perfect should look like. She said:

I was spending money hand over fist to make everything look so perfect. I just depended on what I had learned from my mother and the life I had grown up in because I knew that it was societally correct and would impress everybody. You know, the engraved invitations and everything in silk and taffeta, the handwritten menus, the right band, the right champagne. It wasn't me. After the wedding I felt an immense sense of self-betrayal because the wedding was not an expression of us but an empty event where everything looked perfect.

When a bride finds herself using the word *perfect* at every turn, she might benefit from asking herself why. Is she enjoying the process of organizing her wedding plans as an expression of love, as did Anna? Or is the expectation of perfection creating more chaos than serenity? And while it is important to sort out external matters, this task is secondary to tending to the inner realms. External order can clear the outer clutter and free the space to focus within, but it cannot in itself replace the introspection that is so necessary before the wedding day.

The more significant task is the inner sorting that goes on. Although Psyche was asked to sort actual seeds, these seeds are symbolic of a task that must ultimately occur on the inner level if a woman is to move into her next phase of development. When a woman is on the threshold of marriage and on the verge of stepping into a new identity, she is given an opportunity to assess who she has been within her current identity as well as who she will become as a wife. All transitional times afford us the opportunity to redefine who we are; when we are in between identities, we become like a blank slate on which our past, present, and possible future are illuminated. The task is to take the time, through writing, talking, or simply being, to sort through the areas of our lives that we would like to discard and focus on those that we would like to carry with us. The task is to think honestly about all the components of our singlehood so that when we grieve the identity we take with us the qualities that we would like to uphold and let go of the rest. This process was brought into focus for Helen when she started to design the guest list:

I realized how different the different aspects of my life have been. It's causing me to go through my teens and twenties and think about who I was in all those contrasting areas. This time is bringing it into clear focus, like I am being given the opportunity to take with me the aspects that I have liked from each time in my life and leave the rest behind.

The quest for perfection can also be understood through a spiritual lens. Is it possible that this feverish quest to create a perfect day springs from the desire to create a godlike state for one's wedding? When people strive for perfection, they are striving to attain an inhuman state where only spirit resides. In many ways, the wedding does recreate the luminous world of the spirit. Garlands of white flowers guard the pews; white chairs sit like unfolded angels on a green lawn; light streams in through glass windows, lending an ephemeral air to the setting; bells ring; the bride, veiled and dressed in white, drifts down the aisle holding a bouquet of white flowers. Witnesses are moved to tears by the sheer beauty of the bride and her surroundings. They often gasp, a sign that they are in the presence of the divine. There are few spaces in life where purity, beauty, and light fill the air with such exquisite refinement and where time seems to stand still in reverence of the sacred. Woman and man are transformed, for a moment, into the heavenly bride and groom.

For this brief moment, the bride and groom are elevated to a spiritual state. For a slice of time, they cease to be man and woman and are embodied by the feminine and masculine faces of god. In the Jewish mystical tradition, the feminine aspect of god, called the Shekhinah, is often envisioned as a Bride or Queen, while the messiah is seen as a groom or king. The wedding of these two forces signals the end of days, or the coming of the messianic era. The Christian tradition knows the feminine side of god as Sophia. She also appears as a bride or queen and, according to Woodman (1990) is exalted for her purity of love: "Because she receives perfectly there is in her no stain. She is love without blemish, and gratitude without self-complacency. All things praise her by being themselves and by sharing in the Wedding Feast. She is the Bride and the Feast and the Wedding" (160).

On her wedding day, especially during her ceremony while she stands as a vessel of quiet reception, the bride is filled with the spirit of Shekhinah, Sophia, or any other feminine deity. The creation of a sacred and pure space invites these energies out from within the dusty chests into which we often place them. And those who watch are touched by the gods of long ago.

But there are other gods that are not invited to this scene of spiritual luminosity. The wedding, with its white flowers and sense of awe, is oddly reminiscent of another rite of passage: the funeral. A truly perfect state is not possible without the presence of its opposite; the wedding, this celebration of life, is incomplete without a proper celebration of its partner, death. It is interesting to note that several classic wedding stories include an element of psychological or metaphorical death. Two such tales, *The Chemical Wedding of Christian Rosenkreuth* and *The Parabola*, written in the fifteenth and seventeenth centuries respectively, include graphic representations of death at the wedding: In the former a man is beheaded at the wedding and in the latter the wedding bed is a prison in which the young man and maiden die (Godwin and McLean 1991). These stories acknowledge that the wedding is a day of death and rebirth as both partners die to their current identities before they are reborn. They also portray that only when death is acknowledged can completion, the human equivalent of perfection, exist. But the modern bride, brainwashed to believe that matching teacups and extravagant table arrangements translate to a perfect day, forgets that loss and death figure prominently into this time. Sometimes death only wants a simple acknowledgment of its presence, and when it is ignored, it slithers in through any available opening.

In a culture that fears and shuns death, it is not surprising that the links between funerals and weddings have been erased. The link is alluded to in popular culture—the sit-com depicting the best man who jokes to the groom that he's about to die as he dresses on the morning of his wedding—but we will not find any direct links consciously represented on the wedding day. Still, whether or not we honor death's presence, it still exists, and does not need to be something we fear. On the contrary, the more we embrace the elements of loss and sacrifice, fear and loneliness, the more fully we can embrace the full powers of our beauty on the wedding day. When woman and man stand at the altar as representations of the heavenly bride and groom, they are calling upon the spiritually perfect state that many believe exists after death. This may be an underlying motivation for the bride's urge toward perfection. Some part of her knows that on her wedding day, for at least a moment, she and her beloved will transcend the earthly realm and experience spiritual perfection. And if she's going to be a goddess on her wedding day, she'd better be dressed for the occasion!

The Wedding Dress

The wedding dress is both a mythological and spiritual symbol of perfection. When seen through these lenses, the dress can carry both the princess/queen energy of myths and the goddess energy of true spirituality. When a woman searches for her wedding dress she is searching for the Psyche aspect within her: the pure virgin, the silk-petaled lily, the delicate drop of dew. The gown is the primary symbol of maidenhood during the separation phase and brides will go to immeasurable lengths, often stepping far beyond practical boundaries, to purchase the "perfect" dress. A woman wants to be a princess on her wedding day, adorned in the most beautiful gown she can find as she prepares to meet her prince. To be a princess is to be a character in a fairy tale, and when we tread beyond the superficial reading of fairy tales and view them as signposts to the soul, we can understand the princess as the consummate symbol of innocence, virginity, purity, and maidenhood. The desire to embody these qualities signifies a craving for a restoration of innocence, to become the blank slate on which the transformation into queen occurs. Essentially the wedding dress symbolizes both the untouchable purity of a princess and the regal perfection of a queen. When a woman says, "I want to feel like a princess on my wedding day," she is expressing an impulse to be exalted into the magnificent beauty of the princess and to exude the impression of an otherworldly goddess. When a woman understands that on her wedding day she is elevated to a spiritual state where her transformation can occur, the wedding dress ceases to be merely an object that will help make her "look perfect" but rather can be utilized as an amulet to assist her during her rite of passage.

Stepping into a traditional gown can impart a mythic sensibility, as if one is suddenly graced with the qualities of a fairy-tale princess. Sophia wrote about the feeling:

When I tried on my first real wedding gown, I felt like a princess. Suddenly, the entire wedding came into focus, as if all of the intangible planning for the day crystallized with this singular act. I looked in the mirror and saw a bride. I thought to myself: I am a bride, this is my wedding, this is all very real. I caught my mother's eye in the mirror to see if she was also transported by the reflected image. We both smiled. "I am a bride," I said to her. "I know," she replied.

When Sophia finally found the gown she would wear on her wedding day, she felt restored. She knew immediately that this was the one, that it was "perfect." In this sense perfect can mean "that which precisely reflects a woman's sense of her core-maiden self." Many women felt as if they were putting on a layer of their skin when they found their dress, which often differed from their preconceived notion of the type of dress they would buy:

Sara: *When I began searching for my dress, I had no idea what I was looking for. Unlike many women, I had not spent weeks thumbing through bride magazines gathering ideas that would eventually culminate in the final vision of my gown. In the only wedding I had attended during my adult life, the bride wore a straight, cream-colored, antique dress that she had bought for three hundred dollars at a vintage clothing store. She looked beautiful, and the frugal side of my personality was attracted to the reasonable dollar amount. But when I tried on a used, nontraditional dress it felt musty, weightless, and average. It was then that I realized I had no choice but to walk down the aisle in a traditional gown. I surprised myself with my insistence on abiding by tradition, but like so many aspects of the wedding, I felt guided by something greater than myself.*

Kirsten: *I imagine feeling like a princess on that day—and that's what I wanted in my dress. What I had in mind was short sleeves, on the shoulder and I walked out with long sleeves, off the shoulder.*

Joanna: *I went in and tried on my dress and there was something about the way it felt and hung that felt good . . . . I felt like it was perfect for me.*

Diana: *I tried on many kinds of dresses that probably looked better on me, but when I tried on the dress . . . [starts to cry] . . . my sister was there and she just burst into tears because the dress I wore completely spoke to how [my husband] made me feel . . . It was very young . . . very young and innocent and very romantic, very fresh.*

In the mythological sense, every woman is a princess inside. And on her wedding day, in the spiritual sense, she rises into a queen.

The Princess and the Queen

To *strive* for perfection is human. But brides should ponder this quote by Marion Woodman (1982): "perfection belongs to the gods: completeness and wholeness is the most a human being can hope for" (50). In many ways, the wedding is a fairy-tale day of princesses and princes, kings and queens, veils and flowers and rings and banquets. Yet in this age of high divorce rates and multiple, conflict-fraught marriages, perhaps people are ready to see beyond the one-sided illusion that misread fairy tales and popular media have drummed into our psyches. As Joseph Campbell writes, "the fairy tale of happiness ever after cannot be taken seriously; it belongs to the neverland of childhood, which is protected from the realities that will become terribly known soon enough" (28).

The wedding initiates the bride and groom into their marriage, and in this way should prepare them more honestly for the trials that await them. When bride and groom vow at the altar to commit themselves to a lifetime of partnership and growth, they do not commit to perfection, but to inner completion. Many women marry with the hope of alleviating internal distress or with the belief that their partner is a cure-all that will banish unhappiness. This is the illusory thinking of an uninitiated princess. When a woman faces the heroic journey where she must feel the grief, fear, and loneliness of her transition, she rises into the thinking of a queen. As queen, with the maturity of the initiated, she views her marriage as a spiritual and challenging path to wholeness.

The princess believes that perfection is attainable; the queen knows that it is an illusory vision that the gods offer as a taste of one's highest potential. The princess believes that one can always live in the exalted state of the spirit; the queen knows that to be human is to be flawed, that she is a creature of flesh and earth and soul, and that to deny this reality is to deny herself the experience of being fully alive. The princess does not allow a single fleck of dirt to soil her gown and turns up her nose at all things messy; the queen tumbles on the ground for she knows that true wisdom lies in the meeting of the princess' heaven and the earthly realm. The princess is untouchable within her castle walls, admired from afar but never allowing others inside her innermost chambers; the queen wheels down her drawbridge and welcomes her king inside (certainly a prerequisite for the emotional intimacy involved in a fulfilling marriage). The princess clings to the illusion of perfection and control, running at mad speed as a way to avoid the loss, fear, and loneliness that dwell within her; the queen chooses to surrender, slowing down enough to feel and attend to her inner world and all that has been set into motion by her impending marriage.

Slowing Down

Many brides would benefit greatly from learning how to slow down and embrace the present moment. There are few events in life as monumental in psychological implication as the wedding. In the ideal scenario, it is an event that will only occur once in a lifetime and in many cases commences a woman's journey into adulthood. Where a woman was once single, she is now an intimate half of a partnership; where she was once a maiden and accountable to no one, she is now a wife and accountable to her husband; where she was once a princess in her parents' court, she is now a queen in her own palace. When she rushes through the event with the energy of perfection, she denies herself the quiet time necessary for a thorough transformation to occur. If a bride were to sit still and turn inward she could focus on the emotions ignited by this transformation.

When a woman slows down, she drops into the original nature of her womanhood. Lulled on the gentle waves of her inner waters, she finds her essence, her instincts, and she knows all that she needs to know. In these hidden, quieter regions, she allows herself to grieve the ending of an aspect of herself and welcome the new beginning. In this place of deep knowing she realizes that within the frantic search for the "perfect" photographer, dress, cake, band, rings, invitations, and food, another search is taking place. It is through this second, quieter quest that the true transformation and wedding occurs. It is where she grieves her death as a maiden, cocoons herself in the silks and veils of the bride, and prepares for her emergence as a changed woman, one who is ready to become a wife.

Dropping into Being

When we encounter a problem or an unusual situation in life, our tendency is to ask, "What should I do?" During the wedding process this question plays precisely into the bride's already activated tendency to "do." I would like to encourage brides to rephrase the question, and instead of asking "What should I do?", ask "How can I be?"; meaning, "How can I be more fully with the emotions and questions that are arising during this time?" Here are some suggestions on how to drop more fully into *being:*

- Be willing to feel everything. Be willing to feel the fear, sadness, anger, grief, confusion, and loneliness that you may experience during this transition.

- Drop deeply into the body. The body is a storehouse of emotions and is constantly attempting to communicate its inarguable wisdom with you. The longer we refuse to listen, the more likely it is that the body will demand our attention through sickness or bodily aches and pains. Take the time to ask the body what it wishes to tell you about this time. You may be surprised by the wisdom in the answers.

- Notice and explore your experience as intimately as possible. Sometimes when we are feeling stuck, a transformation occurs when we are willing to look directly into the core of the situation and report back what we find there. This is the concept behind the healing power of art. When we see ourselves with an artist's eyes, we are truly seeing the depth, range, color, sounds, images, metaphors, music, and gestures of our experience. When a thing is fully seen, it usually transforms.

☘ Talk with people who understand transition and are not afraid to talk about the "dark" sides of life. They may be difficult to find. Many people have not explored their own inner terrain, so consequently they're afraid to listen to others! Common phrases that stem from this stance are: "Oh, don't worry, it will pass soon," or "Look on the bright side," or "Can't you focus on the positive fact that you are getting married!" People can concoct endless ways to attempt to talk you out of feeling what you are feeling. Don't let them. Remind yourself that you are in the midst of a transformational experience, that everything you are going through is a normal and necessary part of this transformation, and that through this rite of passage you are being given the opportunity to redefine who you are and who you are becoming. Keep commending yourself for having the courage to descend into your own underworld and simply *be* with what you find. Keep noticing the tendency to want to *do* something when the emotions become uncomfortable. And it will be uncomfortable. When a creature loses its skin, it feels itchy and antsy for a period of time. You are this creature in the midst of losing your skin.

A final note on perfectionism: A distinction should be made between perfection and high standards. When perfection takes hold, the already-present anxiety of the wedding day increases. It becomes an obsession that removes you even further from the experience of the day. A book on overcoming anxiety and panic disorders by Lucinda Bassett offers, "With perfectionism you are never satisfied. With high standards, you feel proud of yourself and the work that you do. The bottom line is that being perfect is impossible" (63). Having high standards inspires you to create a harmonious day and still allows room for gray skies or a rip in your gown. And without the obsessive quality that characterizes perfection, there is room for other experiences to visit your internal landscape, which inevitably leads to a more thorough and satisfying wedding experience.

Chapter Four

Has Everyone Gone Mad?

It is hard to grow up, to feel the ties so strongly and to know you are in the process of severing them on some deep, irreversible level.

—Victoria

Most of my wedding stress comes from the fact that I have blended families. My parents are divorced and my dad just recently remarried. My question is, how do I incorporate this woman, my stepmother, into the wedding? I've only known her for two years; she hasn't raised me at all. How do I include her without hurting my mom and staying true to what I want?

—Kristen

Our wedding, or my wedding as it is beginning to feel like, is in four months. I feel like I have planned this event from start to finish and have received very little help from my fiancé. I understand that the wedding is typically seen as more the woman's day, but that doesn't make any sense to me. I mean, this is supposed to be our day, we are getting married, and yet it seems like I'm the only one who cares about the details of the day. I know how much he loves me and how happy he is to marry me, but I just wish that we were planning this thing together.

—Sara

The Wedding as Theater

While the bride is struggling to manage the loss, fear, and loneliness inherent to this time, those around her may not be faring much better. When the bride doesn't understand what is happening to her, she often reacts with frustration and irritation. Running from loss, chasing after perfection, she finds herself spewing forth words she never thought she'd hear herself say. Those closest to her are not only startled by the possession that seems to have taken hold of the bride, but they may also be experiencing a strange possession of their own. "It was like we had all become someone else. I felt like we were characters in a theater group enacting a strange play that none of us really understood," said Clare.

Several brides compared their wedding time to a theatrical production. Always a love story, the wedding play vacillates from comedy to tragedy and hits nearly every genre in between. Unless the bride and groom have decided to elope or have planned a small wedding with a group of intimate friends and family, the wedding time *does* resemble a spectacular drama. We have the characters of the play—the bride and groom, the mothers, fathers, stepparents, grandparents, minister or rabbi, friends and loved ones—and the sets, costumes, and scene changes for each act. We have people falling into their prescribed roles even when they never thought they would: the feminist who becomes the quintessential bride, the normally generous father who stomps his feet about the money being spent, the active partner who transforms into a lackadaisical groom, the suddenly ferocious mother-in-law. But unlike an actual play where the actors follow a predetermined script, the wedding drama acquiesces to no such order. The participants are asked to improvise, and are given few guidelines on how to understand their spontaneous, and often disturbing, eruptions. The drama of this event will affect not only the stars of the production—the bride and groom—but also the supporting cast, which includes anyone intimately linked to the bridal couple. For although the modern *marriage* primarily exists between the man and the woman and not the two families, the *wedding* still includes everyone.

The bride needs those around her to express the emotions that she may be incapable of expressing. Caught between identities and overwhelmed by her transformation, the bride often feels paralyzed by any act other than quiet reception, especially on her wedding day. She relies on her friends, family, and guests to carry out what she cannot. But in order to play their parts, the wedding party needs to know what is happening in the months leading to the day. If the bride is like the star who has forgotten all of her lines, the wedding party is like a group of actors who were never given the script. Without a greater context for everything that is happening, conflicts are all too likely to arise.

As we have seen, the bride is in the midst of a rite of passage that involves a difficult and painful process of separation. But separating involves more than one person, and just as most brides lack the consciousness to navigate through the confusion of this time, so are those from whom the bride is separating also kept in the dark. Fiancés, mothers, fathers, in-laws, and girlfriends are also trying to adjust to the change—mothers trying to let go of their daughters, fathers trying to reconcile the fact that they are no longer number one in their girls' lives, friends trying to accept that the bride will no longer be chatting as freely with them—but without the consciousness of this separation, there's no room for true feelings to be expressed. The entire engagement is a time of *letting go* for all involved, and letting go involves saying goodbye. If we do not know that we are supposed to say goodbye, we do not allow our feelings of grief to surface, and as a result they are often displaced onto the planning. Instead of grieving, we argue about whether we should have chicken or fish at the reception. Instead of letting go, we hold on for dear life—to each decision, to our relationships as we have always known them, and to our identities as maiden and daughter.

The following are examples of common disagreements that occurred between brides and different members of the wedding party. I begin with the disagreement as told through the bride's eyes, and then offer an interpretation that demonstrates how the engagement is a time for separating and allowing the necessary grieving that always accompanies moving on.

Daddy's Little Girl: Bride and Father

Victoria recounted an argument with her father that occurred six months before her wedding. She began by describing their relationship and what he means to her:

My dad is the sweetest man on the planet. He has been my hero for twenty-seven years. He was my favorite man, literally, until I met my fiancé. My dad is the pinnacle of kindness, emotional accessibility and stability, friendliness, humor, and truth. He's held my emotional hand through so much of my growth and development. He was my ally throughout my adolescent battles with my mother, while never severing his ties to her. My dad is one of the nicest people to be around. He's sweet, funny, silly, goofy, profound, thoughtful, helpful, intelligent, interested, compassionate, strong, soft, and protective while bestowing full faith and trust in me as an adult and woman.

I have never yelled at my dad in my life. I can hardly remember even speaking a harsh word against him, which is why the event that happened at our family cabin on the Christmas before our June wedding, while possibly appearing as a minor incident to an outsider, shook me to my core. What happened was that we were in the cabin and my mom was helping with all these wedding details. Then I thought of one thing my dad could do, something small like checking on some addresses. I asked him and he responded negatively, saying something like, "God, Vic, I don't know that I want to get involved in all that." I turned and lashed out at him, "God forbid you should do something to help in this wedding, Dad!" It was the most sarcastic, combative, stabbing thing I've ever said to him. He was hurt by the comment. He got angry at my reaction, but within a few moments he got tears in his eyes and asked how I wanted him to help. We tried to talk it through but it didn't really get anywhere. After an hour my parents left the room and I wrote them a two-page letter of apology, acknowledging their help, contribution, and support. We did get through it but I still shudder when I think about how I lashed out at him.

This scenario epitomizes the common tendency for brides to transfer their pain about separating onto the planning. When Victoria was able to look objectively at the reality of her father's contribution, she saw that he had helped in many ways: paying for the wedding, hosting a dinner with her fiancé's family, and taking her and her fiancé camping for an engagement weekend, as well as being open to talk about anything regarding the wedding since the onset of the planning. Seen in this light, the angry comment made no rational sense. Yet her outburst did not arise from the mouth of a mature, rational woman, but from the pursed red lips of a little girl—the girl who sensed the impending break from her daddy and whose anger masked her well of pain.

With the wedding just six months away, her descent into the underworld of her wedding experience had begun, and no one could do anything to stop it. She had been starting to feel the loneliness that signifies the beginning of the heroine's journey; like Psyche, she had been tied to Death mountain, left there by her parents, friends, and loved ones until her wedding day. She felt alone with the planning of the event which indicated the deeper loneliness of her internal journey. And in that place of loneliness and pain, without the awareness and guidance to bring these emotions to the fore of her consciousness, she lashed out at the one person who had always been there for her: her father. She said in her description of him that "he's held my emotional hand through so much of my growth and development," but this is where the hand-holding must stop. On some level he may have been responding from a deep knowledge of this truth when he told her that he didn't want to "get involved in all that." This was the father stepping away from his girl at a critical moment in her life, leaving her at the edge of a cliff, knowing that it was time she traverse the abyss alone.

It is very painful to leave the comfort and safety of home. Embedded in the transformation from maiden to wife is the leap into the frightening world of adulthood. The wedding is often the event through which a young woman becomes an adult, whether she likes it or not. Even if the woman has been living away from home for many years, the wedding accelerates her movement into mature adulthood. This is a scary move. It means untying another knot that is tethered to the columns of one's childhood house and facing the world on one's own two feet. It is quite common that when a bride goes home to plan the wedding or visit with her family she reverts to the ways of her maidenhood and becomes like a girl again. As Victoria stated, "After a few days at the cabin it is easy to feel like the 'kid' and have my parents feel like the 'adults'. There was definitely a part of me that wanted to be taken care of and helped all the way through the wedding." Victoria's father, most likely responding to an instinctual knowing, refused to participate in this dynamic. He was forcing his little girl to become an adult, and she didn't like it one bit.

After the argument, when she had had some time to think it over, she realized that the anger over this planning detail was a cover-up for the pain she felt at leaving her father. As she said a couple of months later: "It is hard to grow up, to feel the ties so strongly and to know you are in the process of severing them on some deep, irreversible level." She began to recognize the ways in which she was leaving her father's embrace and transferring her primary allegiance to her husband. The more she allowed herself to grieve this separation, the less she lashed out in "irrational" anger, and the more gracefully she could step into her new identity as wife.

The Modern Aphrodite:
Bride, Groom, Mother-in-Law

Kathryn remembered the tension between herself and her mother-in-law during the engagement:

My mother-in-law was so intrusive during the planning. I remember the contrast from how she behaved toward me before Jay and I got engaged and afterward—it was like a faucet had been turned from warm to cold in a matter of minutes. She had never been overly welcoming of me, but she had always been polite and warm, and I knew that she liked me. But after we announced the engagement she started giving off the impression that she didn't want me to marry her son. When she saw that we were serious about getting married, she suddenly wanted to be a part of every element of the planning. She would call about five or six times a week and always ask to speak to Jay, and then rattle on and on about this cake or that caterer. It was unbelievable to me, and scary that Jay listened and didn't set some kind of boundary with her. We've been married five years now and the tension has definitely died down, but it did take a few years. Jay and I have fought a lot about it. It has been a very difficult issue, and it all started during the engagement.

Kathryn's situation is a very common story that is often played out on the wedding stage. This is the classic triangle consisting of the mother of the groom, the groom, and the bride—the triangle we saw enacted in the myth between Aphrodite, Eros, and Psyche. This is the mother who cannot let go of her son, the mother whose grief at "losing" her precious boy is so overwhelming that she becomes somewhat of a tyrant around the planning of the wedding. The planning provides the perfect arena to spill out all of her rage at this insolent young woman who is "stealing" her son. She rants and raves to her son about the ridiculous choices his fiancée is making, about the amount of money she is spending or not spending, about her choice in table settings or food, and anything else she can dig her claws into. The truth is that she is beside herself with emotion and has no understanding of how to manage it. She probably feels a great emptiness at the thought, most likely unconscious, that her son's primary allegiance is shifting to another woman. If the mother has used her son to fill the empty places in her life—perhaps an estranged marriage or an unsatisfying career—now is the time she will have to come face-to-face with these holes.

Instead of looking at her own grief, loneliness, and anger, she displaces all of this onto the plans for the wedding. She feels that the wedding is her last opportunity to avoid the emotions that live inside her. But, as Kathryn states, the intrusiveness did not end with the wedding. All of the emotions she managed to repress during the engagement still overflowed into her son's marriage. The situation finally calmed down when she found some way to release her son from her embrace and accept that he was committed to spending his life with his wife. There would be much less heartache if the mother could recognize—*during* the engagement—her grief over the loss and separation and spend some real time sitting with herself and her feelings.

This triangle serves another function (as triangles usually do). With all the time and energy the engaged couple spends focusing on the troublesome mother they too can avoid confronting their own feelings about the wedding: The groom avoids feeling sadness about leaving "his mother's nest," as well as any feelings of fear about making this lifetime commitment, and the bride avoids the many feelings spawned by the engagement. If the groom were to refuse to listen to his mother's incessant criticisms of his fiancé, the energy of the triangle would dissipate and bride and groom would be forced to face themselves. Yet without the consciousness and rituals that could sustain the well of emotions that exist within both of them, it is understandable that they would instead agree to participate in this type of triangle.

When we avoid facing the emotions during the engagement, they surface in the first years of marriage. Kathryn and Jay struggled with their intrusive mother-in-law situation for many years before they finally were able to face the real issues. In this situation, the real issue was between the mother and son, and as soon as Jay stopped putting all his energy into mediating and diffusing the conflicts between his mother and Kathryn, he began the difficult process of navigating his new relationship with his mother, which included much more separateness than before he married. Again, the wedding sets the stage for the dramas that play themselves out in the marriage. If the groom doesn't learn to separate from his family of origin before the wedding, the problems that begin at this time will continue until they are openly addressed.

That Stepmother

Kirsten talked about her stepmother anxiety seven months before her wedding:

Most of my wedding stress comes from the fact that I have blended families. My parents are divorced and my dad just recently remarried. My question is, how do I incorporate this woman, my stepmother, into the wedding? I've only known her for two years; she hasn't raised me at all. How do I include her without hurting my mom and staying true to what I want? My stepmom already voiced that she wants to be included and we've had some arguments about it. She has said that she's feeling left out. Honestly, I'm a little ticked off because she should not be included the way she wants because she's not my parent! I strongly believe that the people who should be honored are the people who raised me and Dan. I feel that the wedding is just as much my parents' day as it is my day, and I want them to feel honored. To give the same corsage to my stepmom and my mother is an insult to my mom. I've been worrying about everything around this issue, even down to the photography: Who is going to be in what pictures, and how am I going to incorporate everyone? It's really making me feel stressed.

Kirsten speaks for thousands of brides when she relates her concerns around her stepmother. And while her sense that the wedding is a day where those who raised her should be honored is entirely accurate, the degree to which she is focusing on her stepmother indicates that there are deeper forces at play. It is quite common for the stepmother to become an object—like the ring, dress, and other planning elements—onto which the bride displaces her anxiety. The stepmother is the ideal target in that she is close enough to the internal wedding party that she matters to everyone, but far enough away that the bride can shoot arrows in her direction without too much concern about hurting her. In fact, as often happens during transition, old wounds may rise to the surface, and the bride may subconsciously *want* to hurt this woman who stands between her father and mother. Of course, none of this is usually conscious, which is precisely the point. If the emotions were made conscious, the bride would be forced to confront the real issues: either the tension between her parents, the grief that she still carries about their divorce, or her discomfort about how to incorporate this woman, whom she may actually like, into her life. The wedding drama brings all of these issues into focus, and instead of facing them directly, the bride busies herself with superficial, and emotionally neutral, concerns like corsages and photographs.

It seems that we are wired to direct our negative energy at the stepmother. Fairy tales like Cinderella have ingrained into our minds the notion that stepmothers are nasty, evil people whose purpose in life is to make their stepdaughter's life a living hell. Often there is a pattern of tension between stepmother and step-daughter and between the stepmother and mother that transcends the particular circumstances of our lives. This pattern lends itself quite well to the wedding drama and can provide a convenient subplot that diverts the characters from the main story line. It is important to be aware of this so that when we find ourselves enacting the parts of the characters in these fairy tales, we can take a step back and ask ourselves some real questions. When Kirsten thought about it, she realized that the energy that her stepmother consumed was out of proportion to the actual scenario. The anxiety caused by navigating the challenges of blended families was real, but she came to see that her excessive focus on her stepmother was helping her to avoid her feelings of sadness around her parents not being together. Even though her parents divorced when she was seven, the wedding reactivated the sadness that she will probably always feel about that reality. The stepmother often carries the wedding's shadow, and while putting all the difficult feelings onto her may provide temporary relief, in the long run this approach is not beneficial to anyone.

Maids of Honor

Cora remembered the tension between her and her maid of honor before the wedding:

At my bridal shower a month before the wedding, my bridesmaids sat me down and said, "We need to talk to you." I knew that my maid of honor had set this up and I shot her a look. They said, "Cora, we feel left out. You're not giving us enough to do. We feel like you're leaving us out of everything. We have no idea what's going on." My bridesmaids were obsessing about the details of the wedding more than I was—down to what brand of stockings they should wear! I honestly didn't care what kind, just as long as they wore black. And they wanted to know what kind of shoes to wear and if they should all go together to get them. I said, "Whatever!

Black heels, that's it!" I knew that it was really my maid of honor that was behind this. I could see how angry she was. I didn't understand why she was so angry, but it was clear that she had pulled way back from me. We weren't close at all during the wedding planning, and even now, four months after the wedding, it seems like there's a distance between us that wasn't there before.

There is a reason why the bride's closest friends are called her "maids." As discussed in chapter 3, the bride's girlfriends represent her maidenhood, or the world that she is leaving. They carry the symbolism of more than just her single way of life, but of all the memories, stories, sensibilities, and freedom of girlhood. And not only is the bride separating from them, but they are also sensing this separation and feel that they are separating from her. If the actual feelings of loss are not acknowledged and discussed, they often surface as anger. When loved ones are separating, whether through a move, a death, or a psychological transition, they often go through a stage of anger before they arrive at the deeper sadness. Anger, in many ways, is an easier emotion to feel than grief and helplessness. It is an external emotion that is usually directed, or misdirected, at others. To some extent, it is an appropriate response to someone departing from our world, whether the separation is a literal or metaphorical one. Yet eventually the anger, if appropriately expressed, will dissolve into the pain that lies beneath it.

Cora was shocked by the amount of energy her maid of honor was putting into the minute details of her attire, and saddened by the anger that was directed at her. Yet the bridesmaids are subject to the same tendency of every other member of the wedding when they displace their difficult emotions onto the planning. At that moment, the exact brand of stockings and shoes provided the exact distraction they needed to avoid the real emotions. Unfortunately, this approach rarely serves the greater purpose, which is to help the bride move successfully into her next phase of life and help the "maids" grieve their loss. Instead of releasing the grief, it becomes further entrenched inside the anger, which tends to escalate and create even more conflict. So while on some level we think we are avoiding difficulties by focusing on the planning and erupting in anger, we actually exacerbate the already present tension. Sometimes the emotions will find release on the wedding day, as happened with Kirsten's best friend:

As we were leaving the reception, the DJ played a song called "Goodbye," and everyone started crying. Then I started crying. And then my best friend lost it. I've never seen her cry so hard. She was really upset. Saying goodbye was hard, and I think we both felt it in that moment on so many levels.

As often happens on the wedding day among the various cast members, the maid of honor finally broke down and felt the profound sadness of letting go. Neither Kirsten nor her friend understood the level of emotion, but that was irrelevant. The release allowed the two friends to reunite without the mess of ungrieved emotion under their feet when the bride returned from her honeymoon. Cora and her maid of honor were not so fortunate. They are still trying to find their way back to each other.

Bride and Groom

Sara described her anger and resentment at her fiancé for not taking a more active role with the planning:

Our wedding, or my wedding as it is beginning to feel like, is in four months. I feel like I have planned this event from start to finish and have received very little help from my fiancé. I understand that the wedding is typically seen as more the woman's day, but that doesn't make any sense to me. I mean, this is supposed to be our *day, we are getting married, and yet it seems like I'm the only one who cares about the details of the day. When I've tried to share these feelings with Raphael, he says that he's happy to help if I tell him what I want him to do. But I don't want to have to tell him what to do, I want him to come to me with ideas and excitement about the wedding. I know how much he loves me and how happy he is to marry me, but I just wish that we were planning this thing together.*

This is one of the most common wedding arguments. Sara is accurate in her assessment that our culture views the wedding as "the woman's day," but she is also accurate in feeling that this doesn't make rational sense within the context of the modern marriage. Throughout most of human history, the wedding signified the joining of two families; now, in most cases, it signifies the joining of two people. In the past it made sense that the bride and her family assumed full financial and practical responsibility for the event, for as soon as the wedding was over this responsibility was transferred over to the husband. Today this is no longer the case. Women and men generally enter a marriage as equal partners, and as such it might make sense that they would assume equal responsibility for planning the launching pad for their marriage: the wedding.

While some couples do plan the event together, the majority still follow the traditional view that the wedding is the bride's day. Brides often ask themselves: Do men actually care less about the wedding day than women? To some degree, the answer would be yes, but it is crucial not to measure the man's love for his bride by how much he participates in the planning of the wedding. To understand this common tendency, it is important to remember that a man's rites of passage—the times in his life that mark a change of identity—are very different from a woman's. While the wedding for the woman often initiates her separation from her family of origin as well as her leap into mature adulthood, this is typically not the case for a man. Culturally, men are pushed to separate from their parents, especially mothers, at an early age, while women are encouraged to maintain the family ties as closely as possible. By the time men and women become engaged, the woman is separating from her family, while the man is adding to his. As Robert Johnson says, "Marriage is a very different experience for a man than for a woman. The man is adding to his stature; his world is getting stronger, and he has risen in stature and position." In this sense, women and men are diametrically opposed in their internal experiences. So again these difficult experiences become displaced onto the planning: While Sara may outwardly feel angry at Raphael for his casual attitude about the planning, she may also be responding to a sense of confusion about the disparity in their inner worlds. Some part of her knows that while the man who she will meet at the altar is *bolstered* by this experience, she is in some way *diminishing* inside. She is losing and separating while he is gaining and standing more proud. Ultimately they will arrive at the same destination, but the roads they take to get there are radically different.

This is not to say that the man can just show up for the wedding and doesn't need to contemplate the meaning and changes that the marriage will create. As discussed in *The Modern Aphrodite*, the groom may also need to renegotiate his relationships with his parents, especially if the ties were not adequately cut in earlier years. A man may also be struck by his own fears about making a lifetime commitment and will need to acknowledge that he is no longer a single bachelor free to carouse as he pleases. (An attempt to acknowledge this is seen in the modern bachelor party.) But unless the man is the one in the relationship that is more closely identified with his feminine nature, these changes and fears assume a lesser magnitude than they do for his bride. What seems more common is that the next step toward mature adulthood for men arrives with the birth of a child. It is then that they may be confronted with their relationship to their own father and what it means to step into the shoes of responsible manhood. It is then that the full impact of the end of childhood and the commitment to one woman hits them square in the jaw.

If men and women can learn to understand the significant rites of passage in their own and their spouse's life cycles, much pain and confusion can be alleviated. It is only when the bride attaches a story to the groom's actions—"he's not actively helping with the wedding because it's not as important to him, so I must not be as important to him as he is to me"—that trouble begins to brew.

The Final Weeks

As the wedding day nears, tensions tend to rise within all the primary members of the party. Not only are people contending with the stress and exhaustion that a wedding naturally invites—attending to last-minute details, entertaining out-of-town guests, making confirmation calls, finalizing the ceremony—but the internal changes are also reaching a pinnacle of tension. Every element of control that lives within the bride and those around her will be activated during this time to counteract the sense of feeling completely out of control. As Vivian said, "I don't even think of myself as a controlling person, but during those final weeks I felt controlling about *everything.* I was manic." Carmen and Kelsey talked about prewedding conflicts that erupted just days prior to the event. And while the surface conflicts appear to be about tangible, practical issues, the underlying reasons for these arguments were the grief, fear, and confusion that weren't being directly expressed. Carmen shared an event that occurred the day before her wedding:

My fiancé, Darnell, and I specified to our guests that there would be no children allowed at the wedding. We had attended a wedding with kids there and it didn't work out well. Darnell's best man and his wife, Anton and Ginny, had a one-year-old son and they insisted on bringing him with them for the weekend. The day before our wedding I overheard Ginny telling someone that she was planning to sit in the car during the whole ceremony and reception—from 3:30 pm until 10:30 pm. When I heard this I went ballistic. I pulled my maid of honor aside and said, "That bitch! What is she trying to do? How dare she try to control me and my wedding! She's expecting me to cave in and say, 'Oh you poor thing, you shouldn't be out in the car.' She shouldn't put me in that position. I'm the bride." My fiancé's family had never seen me this angry before. I was trying to explain to them that I felt like I was being controlled and that this was my day. I was willing to make a big scene on my wedding day if she brought the baby inside. But her husband had a long talk with her and she ended up staying at the hotel for the day.

Carmen's story precisely illustrates the tendency for brides to want to control the external elements of the wedding when their inner world is turbulent, especially in those last days. A few days prior to this event, her control issues surfaced with her fiancé around the finalization of the programs. Darnell had assumed responsibility for this task but when she saw what he had done she chastised him, "You're doing it all wrong! You can't do it that way!" Of course Darnell was upset by this and pointed out that she couldn't relinquish control around any aspect of the wedding. She realized that she was becoming irrationally rigid but she didn't know how else to handle what was happening. Again, control is actually a mask for feeling out of control, and when people feel out of control, their emotions become inflamed. In this highly charged state, every decision assumes monumental importance. Brides can relieve some of their anxiety when they put their emotions into context and remember that they are focusing on something tangible to avoid their sense of losing control internally. It is not the program that matters so much to Carmen as the feeling of slipping away from her current identity and the life that she has always lived and the fears she may have about making a lifetime commitment.

During these last hours before the wedding day, the bride is caught in an enormous wave. She is being buffeted by forces much stronger than herself and over which she has no control. When the grip of control seizes the bride, there is only one solution: surrender to it, just as she would surrender to the strength of the wave. It is at that moment, when chaos has flared up all around her, that she needs to sit down in the middle of it all and instead of grasping for control, which will only exacerbate the force of the wave, do the very thing that she refuses to do: give up control. She may not know what she is feeling; she may not have any solutions to the problems that are exploding around her; she may have to accept less than "perfect" programs; but at least she will arrive at her wedding day with a greater serenity and with space inside of her to breathe.

Kelsey shared her prewedding stresses:

My fiancé and I felt pretty fed up with everyone right before the wedding. His family was getting upset with him, and tension was rising all around. Adam got in a few fights with his mom—there was a lot of anxiety about his mom seeing his dad because they don't get along and it was a messy divorce. My dad's girlfriend was going to be there and we were all staying at the same hotel, which was pretty small. My mom was yelling at me about something. We fought about details of the planning that we had disagreed about. My dad got upset and started blaming me because he wanted to be more involved and he felt like he was a guest. The day before the wedding, things got so bad that I was ready to say, "Forget it. Let's go to Vegas." It was that bad. I was so tired of everyone being angry.

Kelsey's story typifies many brides' experiences in those final days. After the event Kelsey was able to talk to both her parents about what had happened. Her mother said that she was feeling very sad about losing Kelsey, but that she hadn't been aware of those feelings at the time. Her automatic response to this grief was to pull away from Kelsey and throw herself into the practical end of the wedding. This was obviously very painful for both of them. The distance between them continued into the wedding day and didn't find resolution until Kelsey returned from her honeymoon and the two were able to discuss what had happened. Her mother felt deep regret that she didn't have the awareness that would have allowed her to say goodbye to her daughter in a conscious, loving way. Instead, she wound herself into a frenzy to keep the difficult feelings, which she felt were inappropriate, off the wedding stage. The truth is that there are no more appropriate feelings to have, and both would have benefited if she had welcomed them onto the stage. Kelsey then asked her father why he confronted her with such harshness the day before the wedding, and the reasons were essentially the same. He also didn't understand the level of sadness he was feeling and only knew that he felt "left out." As for the tension between Adam and his mother, they were never able to talk about it. Clearly the wedding brought into focus the still painful and awkward feelings for everyone about his parents' divorce, and instead of talking about these feelings directly, they expressed them via misdirected anger.

Kelsey's comment, "Let's go to Vegas," is a thought that crosses many brides' minds during the final weeks. In fact, perhaps the most common wedding arguments arise because of the conflicting desires of the bride with whoever is planning (and paying for) the wedding. Tastes clash, egos butt heads, decisions about invitation lists, locations, dresses, and food become a landmine of conflict, and the wedding drama becomes a battle of wills with each contender waving their righteous flags: the bride's flag saying, "This is *my* wedding. I should have it the way I want it," and the mother and/or father of the bride and/or groom retorting with, "Well, we're paying for it and it's just as much our day as it is yours." More than half of the brides interviewed struggled with issues that stemmed from conflicting desires. Jade talked about this issue:

I didn't have the wedding I wanted to have. I wanted to have a very low-key, backyard, bring-your-favorite-dish wedding, and what I got was this over-$10,000 extravaganza. I appreciated the effort and money my mother put into it but I felt disappointed as well. My mother planned my wedding. It started with me but out

*of sheer frustration I gave it over to her. Of course she
was also paying for it, which made it seem like what I
wanted didn't matter. I told her many times, "I want a
free-flowing day on the canals," but that was not
acceptable to her. I felt like my self, from the beginning
of the wedding process, was being compromised. The loss
of self was apparent in that I wasn't doing what I
wanted. And no matter how headstrong I was and how
much I said, "No, no, no, that's not what I want," it
really didn't matter. My mother is a powerful, stubborn
woman, and soon it became clear that the wedding was
not necessarily about Fernando and me but about our
families. The commitment was about us but the wedding
was for everyone else.*

Jade talked about the regrets she felt in the weeks following her wedding that the day didn't more accurately represent the sensibilities of herself and her groom. And yet,
like so many brides, her efforts to assert her will fell flat
under the domineering force of the person paying for the
event.

Cora also felt burdened by her mother's overbearing
presence around her wedding, and this burden carried over
into her relationship with her fiancé. Like some men today,
Anthony wanted to participate in the planning of his wedding, but all of his opinions were immediately sideswiped by
his future mother-in-law. This resulted in Cora feeling pulled
between the two people she cared most about in her life. A
few months before her wedding, she said:

*Whenever the subject comes up, we start fighting. He has
his own ideas about the way he wants to do things and
they clash with my mom's ideas. He doesn't understand
why all these other people's opinions about our day
matter more than his. I try to explain to him that it is*

*our day but my parents feel like it's their party. My mom
says to him, "This is the way you need to look at it. The
reason why it goes this way is because we're paying for
it." I do understand the way he feels—I mean, it is his
wedding—but there's not much we can do about it. It has
put us in an uncomfortable position where we have had
to give up certain things that are important to us and not
have the wedding that we would have ideally wanted to
have.*

While the bride may feel grateful that her parents have
offered to pay for the event, she may need to weigh the pros
and cons of accepting the gift: Are they offering it without
strings attached or do they expect to have a prominent say in
all decisions? By accepting the gift and allowing her family to
plan the wedding, is the bride indirectly communicating to
her family that they will be intimately involved in the couple's marital life? A bride should understand that the wedding can set the precedent for the way decisions are handled
in the future. Even if the bride and groom had been living
together for many years prior to the wedding, the wedding
itself can signify a break, or separation, in the relations with
the family of origin. If the bride decides to allow her parents
to plan the wedding while overriding her groom's opinions,
what message does this convey to the groom? When the
groom's opinions are continually slighted, he will most likely
feel like a third wheel at his wedding and will enter the marriage with the belief that his wishes are inferior to those of
his bride's family. This can set the stage for years of
enmeshed relationships, or result in the continuation of med-
dling that has been occurring for years.

It may be helpful to weigh these considerations prior to
accepting the gift of paying for the wedding. A gift can
express the parents' wish to latch on tighter to their departing daughter or can be given unconditionally as a token of

farewell. If the bride and groom sense the former, they may choose to forego a large event and instead plan a smaller, intimate wedding that reflects the values of their relationship. Vivian had hoped to find a way to take care of everyone's needs without too much self-sacrifice. She knew that she would feel caught between the contrasting desires of those involved in her wedding and fantasized from the beginning about having two weddings:

When we first got engaged I said to Jared, "Can we elope and then have a huge party?" My idea, and I still wish we had done this, was to have had a beautiful, intimate ceremony just between the two of us, then have the proper reception where we would cut the cake and do all the traditional things. But our families really didn't like that. His mother was a recent widower and my parents had recently divorced so we felt like we needed to do this for everyone else. I still have regrets about not honoring my original feeling. I had a very strong sense that the ceremony was for us—to the point where I didn't want anyone to hear us say our vows—and that the reception was more of the public sharing and statement.

When a bride compromises too many of her true desires for her wedding, she often feels a profound sense of self-betrayal in the weeks following the event, as was the case with Vivian. Throughout the wedding day she felt that each act—walking down the aisle with her father, saying the vows in front of everyone—was done for others' enjoyment. She felt like she was playing a role that she would not have chosen and went through the motions feeling lifeless. After the wedding she resolved to listen more closely to her needs and weigh their importance against the needs of others. Only then could she make authentically empowered decisions, instead of decisions that denied her true needs and would lead to self-betrayal. Sometimes the wedding is the event through which a woman becomes more deeply a woman by learning how to speak up for herself and set clear boundaries about her needs and tolerances. As it was for Vivian, it can be a paradoxical situation in that she regrets not having done this for her wedding, but it was the wedding itself that brought these issues to her attention. As painful as this can be, it is often through life's largest events that we learn the most about ourselves. Once again, when we remove the expectation that the wedding has to be a perfect, flawless day and understand that it is a transformative rite of passage, the growth that results from these struggles makes sense.

However, there is a viable, practical solution to the problem of conflicting wedding desires. One bride, Isabel, bypassed the entire conflict by turning the "two weddings" fantasy into a reality. She and her fiancé, Marcus, knew that it would be impossible to have the wedding they wanted as long as their families were involved. Isabel comes from a staunch Catholic, Mexican-American family who would set-tle for nothing less than a large, traditional, Catholic wed-ding for their daughter. Her husband's Irish-Catholic family also insisted that they abide by tradition. Yet Isabel and Mar-cus knew that a Catholic wedding would not reflect their love and commitment. While they both describe themselves as spiritual, neither of them are practicing Catholics, so to have a Catholic wedding would have felt like a self-betrayal and a lie. Yet to disregard their parents' desires would have been unacceptable. They decided that they would have two weddings: a private wedding in the Napa Valley where they would be married by their spiritual mentor in a hot-air bal-loon, and a large wedding to please the families that would follow a year later. Isabel felt it was the best possible deci-sion. As she shared:

Had we not had our own private, intimate wedding in the Napa Valley, my wedding day would not have been enjoyable at all. We needed to do what we needed to do, which meant getting married where and how and when we wanted to. We needed to be able to write our own vows and have the ceremony that we wanted to have. Our mentor created a beautiful ceremony for us. Our vows were things that we could only express in such a small environment. We could not have done that in the Catholic church. I barely had anything to do with planning our big wedding, which was fine with me and fine with both of our mothers! They got to plan the wedding of their dreams and we didn't care because we had already had our day. When our big wedding arrived I felt like I was going to be in a play—that's they way I kept looking at it! And because we had already had our wedding, I didn't have any expectations for that day. The details of it were irrelevant to me. Our first wedding was the ceremony that spiritually merged us and the second wedding was like a performance for others. You put on your costume, you know your lines, everyone plays their part, there's a set in the background. So many people get caught up in where people sit or some problem with the cake—in the drama of it. And I didn't really care about that stuff. The key was that I didn't have expectations for the day, which allowed me to really enjoy it.

If bride and groom feel drawn to create a ceremony that precisely reflects their love while also allowing their families to celebrate their union, this solution may work for them. The bottom line is that the wedding is the launching point for the marriage and it is important to have a wedding that you and your groom feel good about. Sometimes the only way to achieve this is to have two separate weddings.

Rites of Separation Revisited: Separating from Fiancé

During these final weeks, the escalating tension between the bride and groom can also explode. For Carmen, these tensions crystallized around finalizing planning details, when she yelled at her fiancé about the programs. For Joanna, the wedding planning illuminated personality differences between her and her fiancé that became more pronounced just before the wedding. Through the planning process they discovered a basic difference that would affect many aspects of their relationship: He was more of a planner and she was more spontaneous.

For the first time in our relationship we started experiencing conflict. Peter wanted all this structure around everything and I was saying, "Oh, let's just wait. Let's leave it open." We had a lot of trouble with that. We tried to stay open and find compromises, accepting who we each are as individuals. But just before the wedding, the conflicts soared again. Peter was upset with me when the things that I had wanted to leave open didn't pan out, or caused us last minute stress. And I was upset with him for getting so bent out of shape about things! It was scary to feel that way just before the wedding.

Joanna had the sense that she and Peter were being tested, that through the engagement process all of their issues were brought to the surface and magnified. Earlier in their engagement, they had confronted issues around their religious differences. As Joanna explained:

I'm Catholic and he's Protestant. In today's world you don't think of that as being much of an issue but Peter and I are both pretty devout in terms of our respective faiths. One of the biggest questions was how we would raise our kids. We spent a lot of time talking about this issue and knew that it was important to arrive at an agreement before we got married. At first the issue seemed impossible to resolve. I felt tremendous inner turmoil about it and wrestled with it for about six weeks. We just continued to pray and be open. We felt more and more led to stay together and we had faith that we would work this out.

At the end of this six weeks, they arrived at a decision that felt good to both of them. As difficult as it was to face these issues amidst the high excitement of being engaged, they both agreed that it had to be done. They realized that marriage was for life and, as much as they loved each other, they wanted to be sure before they wed that their differences were not irreconcilable. But just when they overcame that hurdle, the differences in their planning styles emerged. And before the wedding their arguing escalated. Again, they felt tested. And again, through trusting in their love and staying open to each other's differences, they passed the test.

It can be nothing short of terrifying to feel anything other than pure bliss just before you are about to enter into a lifetime commitment. The illusion around the wedding tells us that during these final weeks we should find the bride and groom floating in their wedding enchantment and basking in their rosy love. Yet the reality is that transitional times bring all issues to the surface, and the feelings between bride and groom range from stilted tension to full-blown fights, from a quiet separateness to a tingly love. It is not that the engaged couple has lost sight of their love and never experience bliss in these last weeks; on the contrary, the love that brought them together is often reignited during this time. But this is not the whole story. It is misleading and ultimately damaging to believe that the prewedding time, or any time in the marriage, should be *only* blissful. The more we normalize and contextualize the tension, separateness, or anger that arises and give these feelings room to exist, the more likely it is that the love and ease will also return. It is also important that we understand the context in which the anger and numbness exist. This context helps alleviate the "there's something wrong with us" belief that follows on the heels of the disagreement. Sophia longed for a way to understand the negative feelings toward her fiancé that gripped her in the final week. She wrote:

Just before our wedding, a palpable anger toward my soon-to-be husband arose. The anger had been brewing for months, but in that last week it overtook me. I remember battling with it, determined not to allow this unwieldy emotion to tarnish the pure love I felt toward my fiancé, but I lost the battle. I felt annoyed by his presence. I did not want him to kiss me, to touch me, to breathe too close to me.

If I couldn't get rid of it, I could at least learn from it. I asked myself a lot of questions: Was I reacting against the "institution of marriage"? Was this my body's way of responding to an archaic way of life that has entrapped women for centuries? Was my anger the outward expression of an inner fear that I would lose my individuality within our marriage? Was I angry because I felt forced to reconcile these questions alone? Yes, all of this was true. My anger was compounded by the fact that I did not want to be feeling this way just days before our wedding. But as much as I took time and space for myself and discussed my feelings with my fiancé, the anger still remained.

What I remember wanting, even though it was highly impractical, was to spend that last week in silent retreat.

I felt like I needed to be alone in order to prepare for this commitment.

Anger is the body's way of communicating a need. For Sophia, although she felt she couldn't act on it, the need was to take real time away from the man she was about to marry. In fact, Sophia was beautifully aligned with an inner knowing that told her that before she was going to unite, she needed to be separate. On some level, she felt that her time as a single person in the world was coming to a close, and her anger was her body's way of creating distance between herself and her soon-to-be husband to help her to negotiate this transition. She felt the final layers of her singlehood being stripped away; she felt the loss inherent to this rite of passage.

It might seem odd to think about separating from the person with whom you are about to join, but our culture actually includes a tradition that honors this natural impulse: spending the night before the wedding and the wedding morning separately. Traditionally, bride and groom are not to see one another for a sustained period before they meet at the altar. This creates the cocoon inside which each can shed the final layers of their current identity before they become wife and husband.

Just prior to the wedding, the bride enters the liminal phase of her transition, or the in-between state where she is no longer single and not quite married. This state extends to either side of the wedding day. It is the empty space inside which her transformation into wife occurs. Without the space that honors this transformation, she often lashes out in anger at the person she loves most in the world. The final rite of separation that she must endure is not from her mother, her friends, or even herself, but from her fiancé. Brides usually find some way to take this space. If anger is not her style she may busy herself with the planning or become very quiet inside. Helen experienced the separateness as a block between herself and her fiancé. Two weeks before her wedding she said, "It's still us but it feels different, and it's because of all this stuff in my head. It's not a negative feeling toward him, not even anger, it's more that I can't feel anything, like a numbness. It feels so strange." This numbness characterizes the liminal phase. It is the woman's final shedding of identity before she steps onto the stage as bride and ultimately becomes a wife. As with every other aspect of the wedding, the more she can allow it to exist as fully as possible, the more quickly it will pass, and the more likely it is she will arrive at her wedding day prepared and serene.

Questions to Contemplate

🐿 What are the main conflicts that have arisen during the engagement? With whom have these conflicts taken place? Think about the story line of the disagreement, then take some time to see what lives beneath the story line. What emotions are the conflict masking? For example, if the conflict is around your stepmother, ask yourself: What energy is she carrying? What needs to be grieved that she is masking?

🐿 As happened with Kelsey and her parents, when loss is not consciously grieved it contorts into control, anger, or distance. If you sense that someone close to you is masking their loss through these defensive methods, create time in which you can explore the deeper layers of their experience. Even if you do not have this sense it still may serve you to create this time for you and those from whom you are separating, allowing room for the more vulnerable emotions to surface.

🐿 Who is your wedding for? Are you adhering to other people's standards or are you staying true to yourself? Think about any areas where you are allowing your decisions to be dictated by other people's or society's desires. Are there any decisions about the day that give you an uneasy feeling when you think about them (usually an indication that we are not listening to ourselves and speaking our truth)? Are you following your own heart about: your dress; the size of the wedding; the place of the ceremony and reception; the flowers; the colors; the food; the ceremony?

🐿 Have you noticed any changes in your relationship with your fiancé since you got engaged? Have you noticed an increase in anger and resentment toward him? If so, how have you handled these feelings?

Have you felt a need to take extra time away from your fiancé? If so, how can you attend to that need?

Chapter Five

The Wedding Day

I think the reason why a lot of the magic happened is because we didn't wait until the last minute to try to get spiritual. That was my point when we first got engaged. I knew then that it was too much pressure to try to get as deep as you can be on that one day. You have to lay the groundwork. You have to prepare on all levels: practical, emotional, psychological, spiritual. And then you have to be willing to let go of the planning and allow anything to happen.

—Victoria

I was spinning above myself, nearly out of my body and trying desperately to force myself back in. The wedding video reflects what was happening within me: I looked frail and gaunt, my chest heaving in great efforts for breath, like a tiny bird. I had never experienced such sensations. I was alarmed. Would I really faint at the altar?

—Cassandra

I remember I didn't want to take my dress off. It was sort of a Cinderella feeling, like if I took off my dress, it meant it was all over, and I didn't know how to do that. I couldn't take off my dress like it was an ordinary dress, because I knew I would probably never put it on again. It was like peeling off a layer of my skin.

—Diana

A Microcosm of Life

At last the bride, her groom, and their families arrive at the wedding day. This is the day for which they have been preparing for the last several months. It is the culmination of the pain and confusion about separating, the quest to create perfection, the madness that consumed everyone during the final weeks, and, of course, the love and commitment between the bride and groom. There are few events in our culture onto which so much energy is placed. In most cases, the wedding will occur once in a woman's lifetime, so it is understandable that the bride would want this one day to surpass all others in terms of the presence of beauty, joy, and love. The common desire is for her to be more beautiful that she has ever been; for the couple to feel their love more intensely than they have ever felt it; for her to glide like a princess throughout the day; and for her to feel exalted by the outpouring of love that surrounds her from friends and family. Our cultural expectations about how the wedding should look and the bride should feel supersede those of any other time of the bridal journey. Brides enter their wedding day feeling that it should be the best day of their life, and if they experience anything less than this standard, they leave the day wondering what went wrong. As with the proposal and engagement rings, women's responses to their wedding day ran the gamut from disappointing to ecstatic, from calm to devastated.

Kirsten said of her wedding day:

I feel like it was the happiest day of my life. Overall everything went so well and everybody enjoyed themselves. People commented that there was a lot of love and support. The anxiety that people thought would happen with the exes wasn't there at all—the focus was on Dan

*and me. And I did feel like a princess. I had had some
anxiety about my dress on the wedding morning. I
actually really freaked out about it because one of the
shoulders was poofing out. The dress wasn't perfect. Of
course no one noticed it but me. Before the ceremony I
looked in the mirror and I felt strange. I didn't know
why. It wasn't that I didn't like what I saw, but I
thought I would look different. But during the day I felt
beautiful. I know that Dan and I looked our best. And
the dress did fit like a glove—people even commented that
the dress was made for me. I just think I had really high
expectations. And everyone else had expectations of us
looking our best. During the wedding I didn't think about
the problems from the morning at all. I just felt really
happy and present.*

When people ask Vivian about her wedding day, she
says:

*I tell them that I don't remember much of it. I say it
was an awful, stressful day. The truth is that it was a bit
of an out-of-body experience. I didn't have that poignant
moment with my mother zipping up my wedding dress. In
fact, I was helping my mother and sister dress. I was like
a robot saying, "Come on everybody, we've got a wedding
to go to, let's go." I was very quiet, almost in a bad
mood. At that point I just wanted to get through it. It
was a marathon wedding. I felt like I was working. The
ride out to the church was the worst hour of my life. It
was so tense. Then, as I'm walking down the aisle, I see
my parents, who had recently divorced, sitting next to
each other and my father is leaning away so he's as far
away from my mother as possible. It was awful.
Everything that could have gone wrong, did, and I felt
miserable most of the day.*

Victoria, on the other hand, feels blessed that her wedding day far exceeded her expectations. She treasures the day and many of the events leading up to it as some of the most beautiful experiences of her life:

It was a truly perfect day. It was one of those days where time stops and spirit takes over. I've never felt such pure joy and rightness of time and space. We did a lot of preparation to make the day what it was. The practical planning was very important, but the spiritual side was also extremely important, and I knew that we had to plan for that as well. I had had rituals that prepared me on all levels, starting with my bridal shower. My fiancé and I had had rituals once a month during our twelve-month engagement that had to do with the twelve principles that we wanted to incorporate into our marriage. We had put a lot of time and thought into the spiritual side of our engagement and wedding and it paid off in gold. I didn't have to think about it on our wedding day; I could just experience the truth of it.

The ceremony was divine. I felt completely connected to God and to my fiancé. I really listened to the officiator as if he were channeling words from a higher source. My maternal grandfather had died about nine months before the wedding. At his funeral, when my fiancé and I threw dirt on his grave, we looked up and the sun beamed out shining bright. We asked my grandpa to come on the wedding day in the form of the sun. We had the wedding outside and everyone was nervous about the weather—it was in northern California, which doesn't always have sunny weather in the summer—and right before the ceremony the sun beamed through. So during the vows I felt my grandfather there. There was a lightness, too, a joviality in the ceremony. I felt everyone with us. All the things you would want to happen, happened.

I had planned the things that were going to occur during the reception and then we actually went off-schedule! It just worked and I didn't care anymore. I had planned everything, but on that day I was able to let go of the planning and let things happen. The photos were fun and the food was great and everyone was there enjoying themselves and it was just good. Then we did a really fun thing with the dancing, where the bride and groom sit in two chairs and are like the king and queen of the court and everyone comes up and entertains them. So people just kept coming up and doing crazy things: dancing in front of us and singing in front of us and jumping and being goofy! All these random things. That made us feel like everyone had a chance to let loose, where you're not thinking, you're just being. That's what I always wanted for my wedding, where you're just there, having fun. Sometimes it's hard to make fun happen. I treasure that we were really able to have fun!

I think the reason why a lot of the magic happened is because we didn't wait until the last minute to try to get spiritual. That was my point when we first got engaged. I knew then that it was too much pressure to try to get as deep as you can be on that one day. You have to lay the groundwork. You have to prepare on all levels: practical, emotional, psychological, spiritual. And then you have to be willing to let go of the planning and allow anything to happen.

In many ways, Victoria had the wedding that all women hope for. It is important to understand that, as she said, it wasn't just luck that allowed her wedding to unfold as beautifully as it did. During her twelve-month engagement, she had spent as much time preparing in the intangible ways—those that would not be seen by the guests—as she did in the practical ways. She had allowed herself to grieve, she had come to terms with the end of her singlehood, she had become aware of her expectations of perfection and was willing to let them go, and she had consciously laid the groundwork that would invite the spiritual elements to grace her day.

Cassandra, representing the majority of women, felt the tension, the disappointment, and the joy on her wedding day. She wrote:

My wedding day was nothing like I expected it to be. I felt I had been seduced by the media to believe that my wedding day would be the apex of joy in my life; that I would shine gloriously in my princess gown; that my groom and I would gaze into each other's eyes, brimming with the love and devotion that led us to make this commitment. I thought I would float through the day with ease. While in some ways I was shocked and disappointed by what transpired, in other ways my wedding day far exceeded my expectations. Where I thought I would feel present, I felt disoriented; but where I thought I would feel ordinary, I felt transcendent. Throughout the day I vacillated between the most extreme emotions: I felt alive, and then I felt absent; I felt calm, and in the next moment everything was chaotic; I felt disconnected from my husband, then we would be gliding on the dance floor enraptured in our private world. Everything was present in a way that I never expected, but I felt more absent than I ever thought possible on my wedding day.

As with the proposal, ring, dress, and every other aspect of the wedding, there is no correct or ideal experience. In the middle of her reception, Cassandra asked her sister-in-law, Lauren, if she had felt like she was in a dream on her wedding day. When Lauren said that that was exactly how she had felt, Cassandra relaxed to know that she was not the only one to experience anything less than ecstatic vitality on her wedding day. The sense of aloneness and confusion that begins for brides during the engagement continues into the wedding day. The sense of unreality or even mundanity that women experience is compounded by the expectation that this is *not* how they should be feeling. Not only are brides relieved to share their common wedding experiences with other women, they are also soothed when they can put these internal experiences into their appropriate context. Just as it is completely normal for a woman to feel grief and fear during her engagement, it is also normal for her to feel both everything and nothing, both clarity and confusion, both presence and absence during her wedding. When these paradoxical emotions enter the bride, she knows she is in alignment with this second phase of her rite of passage.

Because the wedding is a day of transition in which the bride is between identities—no longer single yet not quite married—the wedding day becomes like a microcosm of life. In a single, transformative day, all emotions reveal themselves. Our culture typically has difficulty accepting the paradox that conflicting emotions can exist in one event. Occasions like weddings and funerals are seen as either joyous or somber, without room for shades of gray and without the possibility that two or more emotions could live in a single moment. Brides, like Cassandra, are often shocked by the multiplicity of emotions they feel on their wedding day. Our culture does nothing to prepare us for this experience. We think we are supposed to be happy and are confused by the sadness that lurks in the background; we think we are supposed to be more present and more beautiful than we have ever been and do not know how to make sense of our lack of presence at the event. In order to understand this common experience of brides, we need to put the wedding day into the context of rites of passage.

The Wedding: A Day of Transition

On this one day, the woman, through ritual and ceremony, passes from single to married and from maiden to wife, and for the transformation to be complete she often needs to span the spectrum of human emotions. The wedding is a celebration of life and union and also a day of death and separations. It is the funeral for the single woman as much as it is the birth of the wife. She is neither here nor there and, like the lobster without a shell, she drifts through the wedding day without a skin. Her old skin has been shed over the course of the engagement and her new skin has not yet been formed. The wedding is the white flowered arc under which the bride passes to symbolize her transition into wife; it is the bridge over which she walks to signal the death of one way of life and the birth of another.

In his work on rites of passage, Arnold van Gennep (1960) referred to the second phase of rites of passage as transition rites and the psychological state that accompanies transition as liminality. The liminal state is the amorphous time between two distinct states of being. We say that someone is "in limbo" when she is in between jobs, relationships, or any time one state ends and the next has yet to begin. Liminality is at once nothing and everything: It is a time of formlessness in that the initiate stands between two identities without being firmly attached to either one *and* the initiate bows to both the past (life as a single woman) and the future (life as a married woman), thus acknowledging and incorporating two states of being. The initiate is at once *leaving being* and *coming into being* as she waits in a timeless, empty holding space. The holding space can feel like the deserted terrain of a no-man's-land, and can explain the sense of "walking through a dream" that many women feel at some point on their wedding day. The sense of fading in and out of presence is the experience that characterizes the day for brides. Women talked about it:

Kelsey: *I felt like my wedding day was a dream. I look at the photos and it looked like a dream. Sometimes it's all a blur when I think about it. I tried to stay present but it was a struggle. It was overwhelming and chaotic.*

Dana: *Throughout the day I felt of two bodies—I felt split. I felt like there was a part of me that was really calm and present and another part of me was just gone.*

Jade: *I felt present but then I wouldn't feel present. I felt in-between. There was a very dreamlike quality to the day.*

Women felt the dreamlike quality most acutely during the ceremony. Although our culture encourages us to focus our primary attention on the details of the reception, the ceremony is the ritual event that *weds* the bride and groom, and should be understood within this sacred context. It is, in essence, *the wedding*, the act that unites two into one and consecrates their lifetime commitment to one another. It is during the ceremony, especially the first half before the vows are spoken, that women feel the intensity of the spiritual transformation that is occurring. Most brides are grossly underprepared for the gravity of these moments. Rosa said she felt confounded by her inability to stop her knees from knocking together beneath her dress. Joanna recalled feeling like she might faint at the altar. Diana described her experience in this way:

I felt like I was all alone in that church and everybody was just watching me. I could not feel my groom. I could feel my sister a little bit standing behind me, as if she were breathing her strength and support into me . . . I didn't hear any of the vows . . . The rituals were beautiful and old and archaic and I wanted so desperately for them to mean something to me. I had deliberately selected things that were very powerful in the hope that they would act as some kind of elixir, that they would draw me into the moment. But they didn't. I felt lost. I felt like there was a blanket around me.

There are few moments in life when we are catapulted to a realm that defies our normal conceptions of reality, time, and space. There are few occasions when we feel lifted off the ground without the ability to plant both feet firmly below. In the realm of nothingness, when the old identity is relinquished and the new status is still elusive, the bride may feel like she is in a void. Without a skin and in the midst of the liminal state, she is left vulnerable to the spiritual powers around her. In the void where nothing and everything collide, chaos is bound to occur, and to assimilate this chaos, knees will knock together, bodies will feel faint, and limbs will shake. When the bride doesn't understand what is happening to her, she may feel frightened by these normal occurrences of her body. But with the consciousness that she is experiencing a spiritual transformation, she can allow herself to surrender to whatever needs to occur.

Unless a bride understands the ceremony within this spiritual and archetypal context, she will berate herself for failing to maintain utmost presence during this important hour of her life. It is easy to attach meaning to our state of presence during the ceremony, worrying after the wedding that the ceremony didn't achieve what it was meant to achieve. Cassandra spent months after her wedding ruminating about her lack of presence during the ceremony. She described herself during the first half of it as completely overwhelmed:

I was spinning above myself, nearly out of my body and trying desperately to force myself back in. The wedding video reflects what was happening within me: I looked frail and gaunt, my chest heaving in great efforts for breath, like a tiny bird. I had never experienced such sensations. I was alarmed. Would I really faint at the altar?

She had entered the ceremony with several expectations and when she fell far short of measuring up, she wondered what was wrong. Like most brides, she had wanted to feel her groom's love throughout the ritual. She had wanted both of them to feel vibrantly alive and had imagined that she and her groom would stand in their highest selves. She also felt that the ceremony should serve as a well of love and purity that they could drink from in future years during times of strife and emptiness. She wrote about her most troubling expectation, the one that caused her months of turmoil when she thought back on the wedding:

I believed that the ceremony was the point of conception for our marriage. Somehow I had arrived at the conclusion that a vibrant ceremony, in which our love was vividly apparent, would create a strong, passionate marriage. By contrast, a mediocre ceremony would create a colorless marriage. In my mind, the quality of the wedding would determine the success or failure of the marriage. There were positive aspects to the ceremony. I did feel beauty and serenity in the last part, after the vows were spoken, but these positive aspects were overshadowed by my shock and confusion at my inability to remain in my body. For many months after our wedding I felt plagued by questions concerning that first half: Where was I? Why was I so overwhelmed? What had happened to me? Was our marriage doomed to mediocrity because we had not been bursting with life throughout the ceremony? I had wanted nothing more than to feel each precious moment of those forty-five minutes and to feel uplifted by the sacred words and rituals; instead I had felt empty and lifeless.

It is important to understand that the wedding does not determine the success, failure, or quality of the marriage. To maintain a vital marriage is a daily challenge, and while it is wonderful when a woman can look back on her wedding day with joy and serenity, the ceremony itself is not responsible for the daily reality of a marriage. When a bride checks her expectations before the wedding and is prepared to receive anything on that day, the possibility of having a present, positive experience is increased. But with her idealistic mind and a potpourri of popular images, more often than not the bride is left to form inappropriate assumptions for what the ceremony will hold.

Cassandra wrote that after the vows were spoken she felt more present, and that for the rest of the day she passed in and out of presence. She echoes the way that most brides talked about their wedding day: moments of complete clarity interwoven with the fuzzy, dreamy states. As a microcosm of life and a day of transition, it would make sense that the wedding would bring on these vastly different states of being. Most regular days in life include presence and absence, but the wedding magnifies all inner states. In the presence we feel starkly clear and in the absence we feel almost ghostly. It seems that for many brides, the moments of presence were preceded by a release of some sort—the vows, the dancing, crying or laughing—and that these releases occurred after a tense or chaotic situation. Here we find that the wedding day includes another dichotomy:

moving from chaos to serenity and presence, and from serenity back to chaos and absence. This is the typical pattern of the bride's internal landscape. It is the ebb and flow of the old life giving way to the new, the tension and release that precedes any new birth. It is an essential component to the transformation of identity that defines this day.

Pan Rears His Head:
From Chaos to Serenity

Images of the serene bride are a direct contrast to scenes of wedding-day chaos. In fact, stories of disasters that befall the bride on her wedding day have become almost stereotypical in our culture. Yet it is a fine line between stereotype and archetype, and this juxtaposition of chaos and serenity is actually a hallmark of liminality. Liminality is the space in between a death and a new birth. In this space we find both the emptiness of serenity and the clutter of chaos, with both states dependent upon one another in order for the new birth to arise. Martin Buber (1947) wrote on the importance of the liminal state in any process of transformation: "Nothing in the world can change from one reality into another unless it first turns into nothing, that is, into the reality of the between-stage. And then it is made into a new creature, from the egg to the chick. The moment when the egg is no more and the chick is not yet, is nothingness. This is the primal state which no one can grasp because it is a force which precedes creation; it is called chaos" (104).

Again, as with the madness of the engagement, chaos rears its head. One of the keys to finding serenity on the wedding day is the willingness to surrender to the chaos and release the energy that it carries. The more the bride or those around her are able to release, the more grounded she will feel within her body. The more she resists the inevitable chaos, the more outside of herself she will feel. Like the engagement, we are conditioned to believe that the wedding should only include beauty and joy. We ignore the shadow, and when it insists on making itself known, we defend against it through keeping busy or becoming manic about details, simply because we don't know that surrendering to it would help us. The typical wedding day is designed to keep chaos at bay. We are encouraged to make specific timetables about who will be where and what will take place when. These timetables, while attempting to make the day run smoothly, actually invite chaos to the wedding banquet, because it is nearly impossible to abide by these schedules when the wedding day energy is set in motion. No matter how much extra time we allow, somehow chaos manages to creep in and fill all the empty spaces. Let's take a look at the way one bride refused to break down and the consequent displacement she felt on her wedding day.

Cassandra was the quintessentially prepared bride. She had followed all the wedding day checklists and was prepared to step onto her wedding stage with the knowledge that everything would unfold gracefully. She had been conditioned to believe that if she followed all of the prewedding guidelines, everything would progress without a hitch. Of course, she realized that some surprises are inevitable, so she also allotted extra time around key events to avoid being rushed. Cassandra's wedding morning typified the experience of many women. It included the interplay of chaos and serenity that characterizes so many brides' stories. She wrote:

I awakened on my wedding morning at 7 o'clock, excited and expectant. Before I stepped out of bed I wrote in my journal, "I want to seize each moment of the day—believe and feel and breathe into each moment." I spent the morning attending to my personal needs—taking a short walk and preparing a healthy breakfast that would last me through the morning. By nine o'clock I was ready to leave my house, pick up my best friend, Olivia, and drive to the salon where my girlfriends, mother, and I were to have our hair done. The woman who did the flowers was supposed to arrive at quarter to nine to drop off the bouquet, corsages, boutonnieres and, most importantly, the flowers that were to be woven into my hair. But by nine o'clock she still had not arrived. I was beginning to panic. She finally arrived but the bouquet was in the wrong shape and she had brought purple baby's breath for my hair instead of white. I was livid, but I had no time to argue with her.

I had to stop at the market to pick up the white baby's breath, which made me late to everything. I picked up Olivia and we drove downtown to the salon. I was stressed, but as soon as I entered the peaceful salon atmosphere, I relaxed. The morning there was one of the most relaxed, intimate times of my wedding day. I loved seeing all my girlfriends and mother around the salon: my sister-in-law, Lauren, walking across the room in her jeans and brown cover-up robe; Olivia smiling at me from beneath the large, round bowl of the hair dryer; and my mother in serious discussion with the woman styling her hair. I felt calm and centered, fully ready for whatever the day might hold.

Then everything got chaotic again. My hair was taking much longer than I had anticipated and Olivia and I had to rush back home to get ready for the photos. I remember feeling annoyed at Olivia for not driving quickly enough. When we finally got back to my house we hurried into the bedroom, shut the door, ripped off my clothes, threw on my wedding gown, earrings, necklace, *pantyhose, shoes, a dash of eyeliner, a line of lipstick, and I was ready to walk down the stairs that lead into our backyard and meet my groom. Everything was crazy from that point until we arrived at the church. There was not a moment of serenity during the whole photography session. The tension between my parents, who had not uttered more than five words to each other since their divorce three years earlier, filled the air. I felt completely out of my body, watching everyone stressing about the most trivial things—like my mom worrying that the wind was messing up her hair. I was miserable, and from the look in my fiancé's eyes, I could see that he wasn't faring much better. But I kept going. I didn't know what else to do.*

Let's take a look at Cassandra's experience through the lens of liminality. While nothing seriously disastrous occurred that morning, the frenzied pace and confusion about chaos' surprise visits set the tone for the rest of the day. Chaos serves several functions, the most important of which is to encourage the bride and/or those around her to break down and *feel*. Any losses and fears that weren't consciously recognized during the engagement, like the pain about her parents' divorce, would most likely make their presence known on the wedding day. But Cassandra had refused to break down and feel her losses. Her focus was on hitting each wedding mark on time and trying to force herself to look like the beautiful bride she thought she would be. There was nothing inherently wrong with wanting her wedding day to run smoothly, but with every moment accounted for, she left little room for the necessary spontaneity, grief, or madness to arise.

What would have happened if, in the midst of that backyard frenzy, someone had yelled, "Stop!" and they had halted in their tracks and stepped outside of the lunacy that had consumed them? And what would have happened if instead of running around trying to take all the right pictures, they had been willing to feel the losses in the day? Would Cassandra and Olivia had flung their arms around each other, defending against the impending break in their friendship? Would Cassandra have grieved the fact that her parents weren't speaking on her wedding day? Would her father have acknowledged the sadness at "losing" his little girl? Would her mother have shared her feelings about the change that this day would bring to their relationship? Ideally, these conversations would have taken place during the engagement, but without proper awareness Cassandra didn't know that this was a part of her engagement tasks.

In the absence of this consciousness, pandemonium threatened to seize her. The ancient Greeks would have said that she had been seized by the god Pan. Robert Johnson (1989), referring to a section of the myth of Psyche and Eros, describes this figure as "the cloven-footed god . . . the god of being beside one's self, wild, out of control, near-madness, which the ancients thought so highly of and we regret so bitterly when it seizes us. We derive our word *panic* from his name. It is this quality that saves Psyche" (50).

Here we derive wisdom from Psyche. In one of her moments of despair, when Aphrodite gives her an impossible task, she goes to the river with the intention of killing herself. At the river bank she meets Pan, and when she allows herself to be touched by his presence, she is saved. Perhaps if Cassandra, too, had allowed herself to be gripped by Pan, to collapse into the *pan*demonium of that morning, she would have unraveled into the weeping and madness that she was trying to keep locked behind closed doors. And after the grief had passed through her body, she might have experienced the release and subsequent calm that often follows a fit of weeping. But chaos and pandemonium had no place in the controlled chambers of her wedding day perfection. They tried to pull her into the wave, but she would not be taken. Chaos had reared its head at various points throughout the morning, beckoning her to collapse, to break down, to feel. She had written in her journal that morning that she wanted "to seize each moment of the day"; she did not write that she wanted to *be seized*. Like most brides, she did not want to lose control. The consequences of refusing to surrender to madness and grief were that she felt outside of herself. The emotions compressed within her and she became numb. The beauty, vibrancy, and serenity that had graced her earlier that morning had been swallowed within the grief and loss that she had refused to feel.

But Pan offers many chances to break down. After this hectic morning, moments before walking down the aisle, Cassandra's mom brought her back into her body and she finally succumbed to Pan's attempts to break through. She described the moment in the bride's room:

The ceremony was to begin in ten minutes. My girlfriends had been scuttling around me, attending to last-minute details about seating arrangements, fixing their hair, fussing about this and that. Suddenly my mother asked them if they would leave the room. She wanted a moment alone with me before we walked down the aisle. After they departed, the calm of the early morning quietly returned. She turned me to face her. She put her hands on my shoulders. Her eyes filled with tears, and with a broken voice she said, "You are such a beautiful bride—the most beautiful bride there ever was. I am so proud of you. I love you so much." And suddenly the tears that I had refused to shed all morning were streaming down my face. Her words were like an emotional transfusion. At least for the moment, I felt alive again.

In the myth, each time Psyche feels overwhelmed by her situation, Pan appears in one form or another and asks her to collapse. When chaotic energy builds, either it is dissolved through emotional release or the bride suffers from inner implosion. Some moments in life are so large that the only way to remain present, or to flow in and out of presence, is to drop down into the body and allow whatever lives there its fullest expression. The brides and families who felt most miserable on their wedding day were those that refused to acknowledge any loss (like Vivian, who endured the car ride from hell with her recently divorced parents because everyone refused to talk about what was really going on). If the incredible forces of the wedding day are denied, the body shuts down and becomes numb. On the other hand, the brides who were able to remain most present during the wedding day were those who allowed themselves to be seized by emotion, spontaneity, and even a little bit of madness.

The appearance of these losses doesn't need to be chaotic, if they are allowed room to exist. Kelsey remembered that one of her most serene times in the wedding morning was when she was having her makeup done:

The chair was positioned so I was looking out the window in the den. I began experiencing the loss of my parents not being together, and I also felt the loss of my grandfather, who had passed away two years before the wedding. I knew he would have been so proud of me and would have adored my fiancé. I felt serene and calm inside, and said to the makeup lady, "Oh, it's so nice just to look outside." At that moment a bird came and sat on a branch of the tree, and I instantly thought of my grandfather. The bird looked at me for five minutes. I looked back at the bird and let my mind drift to warm memories of my grandfather. I knew he was with me the whole day.

Joanna and her groom, Peter, actively invited loss to participate in their wedding. Joanna had experienced tremendous loss in her life and knew that if they didn't acknowledge these losses at the wedding, there would be no room for joy to blossom. Joanna married at age thirty-one; her father passed away when she was twenty-five, her brother when she was twenty-seven, and at age twenty-eight she lost her mother. Just prior to her wedding she lost her dear aunt and one of her best friends. Through these losses, Joanna learned to express the grief and difficult feelings that arise in the face of death and loss. She developed an understanding of the stages of grief that follow both literal and psychological deaths, and she was able to bring this consciousness into her wedding day. She credits her ability to recognize and feel loss with allowing her to feel joyous and free on her wedding day. As she said:

The fact that my parents were not alive and that I had experienced so much loss touched every aspect of the wedding. At every stage, that was part of the experience of loss—my father would not walk me down the aisle, my mom would not go shopping with me for a wedding dress, they would never see me get married, they would never meet Peter. It had to be reckoned with. As it got closer and we had showers and a rehearsal dinner, their presence was always missed. I had to actively work at allowing myself to grieve the fact that they, and my aunt, weren't there. It was very significant. I was so out of it on the night of the rehearsal dinner. After the rehearsal I went to the back of the church and just wept. That was the point I was the most aware of the losses.

We both felt it was important that we acknowledge the losses during the ceremony. So we had a moment of silence when Peter and I knelt down and the priest said, "As many of you know, there are many people that are

*not here with us today." And in our program we put "in
memory of," then my parents' and brother's names. I
went through a training at the Grief Recovery Institute
and one of the things they said can be very painful when
someone has died is if everyone knows about it but no
one is talking about it. At the reception, both of my
uncles spoke, and they both mentioned my parents and
how happy they would have been. After my uncles had
given the toasts, I took the microphone and said
something like "this is such a happy occasion and it is
also a sad one," somehow acknowledging that my parents
weren't there. I felt that that created the space for those
of us who knew that they were gone to let it out. And
then we just had a blast! We had so much fun. There was
such a sense of joy.*

Through conscious acknowledgment of loss, Joanna
and Peter released feelings that might have escalated into
chaos and instead experienced joy. Feeling those losses
allowed Joanna to be more present for the wedding day. It
rounded out the day for her.

The losses in Joanna's story are more obvious in that
they are literal losses. For most brides, the loss is psychological and in this sense is more difficult to address directly.
Sometimes the bride is so overwhelmed by her transition that
she cannot feel the loss, and she needs those around her to
express what she cannot. Several brides talked about other
members of their wedding party breaking under Pan's touch.

Carmen: *I walked out to take pictures and found my
brother and aunt with their arms around each other
sobbing, like somebody had died.*

Cora: *My groom couldn't stop crying during the
ceremony, which caused the minister to choke up, and
that made me start crying. Before all the crying I felt*

nervous, but I think the tears released the tension and I felt more relaxed after that.

Kelsey: *Before I walked down the aisle, I felt stressed and out of my body. I had been rushed all morning and couldn't find my center. Then I heard the opera singers singing Ave Maria. My entire bridal party started crying, which made me cry and brought me back into my body. That was a release. I said a quick prayer and immediately felt stronger. I thought I would break down while walking down the aisle with my father but instead he broke down. He was sobbing the entire time.*

The intense wedding energy seems to transfer into whoever is most available to receive it, urges that person to collapse, and then moves on. In this way the wedding party also surrenders to the chaos of this transition and helps give birth to the new wife. People may not know exactly what they are feeling or why they are crying, but in the end it doesn't matter. The more we can express everything that arises—the loss, the joy, the nothingness, the feeling of being overwhelmed, the beauty, the love—the more easily the bride can move through this transitional day and step into her role as wife in the weeks and months to come.

When many people gather together, a buzz is created; when these people are gathering for a greater purpose—in this case to witness the formal commitment between two people—a powerful energy is created. Either the energy is acknowledged and expressed, or it implodes and creates more chaos. And where we find chaos, we find Pan. Pan doesn't ask for an invitation to the wedding. He just shows up, and the best we can do is accept that on days of transition, in moments as monumental as the wedding, our most effective choice is to surrender to his ways. A common trap for brides is look back on their wedding day and dwell on the mistakes—not planning enough time, picking the wrong cake, etc. The truth is that no matter how much planning and consciousness goes into the day, there will be "mistakes." And these "mistakes" should always be cradled by quotation marks because they aren't really mistakes at all, but essential moments of the day. They are when Pan breaks through the bride's cool veneer of perfection and beckons her to follow him to the river's edge where she can crumble beneath the wispy, green branches of the willow tree . . . and weep.

From the Reception to the Wedding Night

The first year of marriage officially begins after the vows are spoken. The bride and groom have spoken their commitments and they are presented to the world for the first time as husband and wife. While the bride may continue to feel as if she is in the liminal state for many weeks or even months, all of the events that take place after the vows are part of the third phase of a rite of passage: *rites of incorporation*. To incorporate literally means "to bring into the body"; rites of incorporation are objects and rituals that bring the events of the ceremony into the physical and spiritual bodies of the bride and groom. Van Gennep's research has shown that common rites of incorporation among indigenous people are holding hands, pronouncing an oath, eating and drinking together, kissing one another, and exchanging gifts (rings, garments, sacred objects). About the last category he says, "Exchanges have a direct constraining effect: to accept a gift is to be bound to the giver" (29).

All of the above rites are represented during the ceremony and reception of a traditional wedding: Bride and groom hold hands during their vows; in the Jewish ceremony, they drink wine from a single glass; the couple lights a unity candle from the light of their individual flames; bride and groom kiss; at the end of the ceremony they walk down the aisle together, as opposed to meeting each other from their separate paths when the ceremony began. These acts are all rites of incorporation, intended to merge spiritually two into one.

The reception, although at times heavily cloaked in perfectionistic display, is actually comprised of many rites of incorporation. The guests eat and drink together, and in this sense all become a part of the new union. The rites of incorporation continue throughout the evening: the couple dances together, they link arms as they drink champagne, and they feed each other a slice of the wedding cake. The last ritual takes on particular significance in that a piece of the cake is frozen so that it may be eaten at the one-year anniversary. In this way, the joining together in marriage that began at the wedding finds an element of completion at the end of the first year. The final symbol of transition occurs when the groom carries the bride over the threshold. The threshold symbolizes, in Joseph Campbell's words, "A mystery of transfiguration—a rite, or moment, of spiritual passage, which, when complete, amounts to a dying and a birth" (1949, 51). And at the day's end, the couple consummates the wedding with the final rite of incorporation, setting the seal upon their marriage for many years to come.

Let's talk about this final rite of incorporation, the wedding night! It is unlikely that if the bride has grown up in this culture she can escape having expectations for this night. Even brides who glided through their engagement and pranced onto their wedding day with ease, avoiding all the common pitfalls of expectations, entered their wedding night burdened by thoughts of what should transpire. We imagine, because of what we have seen through the media, that this night is supposed to be the most passionate, romantic, explosive night of our lives. We see ourselves gracefully slipping out of the wedding gown and joining our new husband on a bed covered in rose petals. We fantasize that we will gaze into our husband's eyes and sweep each other into the throes of ecstatic union. The truth diametrically opposes this fantasy. Of the dozens of brides with whom I spoke, only one fulfilled this expectation. Most brides sheepishly shared that they were exhausted and that the sex was, at best, average. Only one bride, Vivian, unabashedly refused to abide by this tradition:

I told my fiancé months before the wedding, "Just so you know, honey, we're not making love on our wedding night." I felt that the pressure was too big and I anticipated our exhaustion. I was also forewarned about the common disappointments about the night. There were so many women, even little old biddies, who took me aside and whispered, "You know, the sex is really bad on your wedding night—don't expect much!"

The most common response to how the bride felt on her wedding night was "exhausted." The exhaustion hit almost the moment she arrived at the hotel room. The discrepancy between the bride's and groom's inner states was also apparent. Most grooms were pumped up and ready to go, while most brides felt like they wanted to sleep for a week. Yet, despite this exhaustion, which on a normal night would have precluded any thought of sex, nearly every bride submitted to the wedding night ritual. They felt obligated on multiple levels to "consummate" their marriage.

Paulina talked in depth about her wedding night. She shared how her husband gallantly swept her into his arms and carried her over the threshold. He was full of life, exuberant, proud; she was exhausted, sad, confused. She said she looked at him and wondered how they could be feeling so different even though they had just experienced the same event. She sat in her wedding gown and wrote in her journal while he changed out of his suit and smiled at his ring. Paulina felt reluctant to take off her wedding gown and prolonged the act as long as possible. She said, "I resisted the act knowing that when I took the dress off my time as bride would end." Several brides described similar feelings. Diana shared:

I remember I didn't want to take my dress off. It was sort of a Cinderella feeling, like if I took off my dress, it meant it was all over, and I didn't know how to do that. I couldn't take off my dress like it was an ordinary dress, because I knew I would probably never put it on again. It was like peeling off a layer of my skin.

Taking off the dress *is* peeling off a layer of skin. It is when the final layer of maidenhood, of life as a single person, of primary identity as daughter, of all the planning and details of the previous months, fall from the bride's body and collect in a silk-satin heap at her feet. With this act the wedding ends. As Paulina said, "When the dress fell from my body, the emptiness that had been with me throughout the day thudded in dull pangs in my belly."

In that state of mind, it is no wonder that making love feels like an obligation. When Paulina's husband approached her tenderly and passionately, she tried her best to convince her body to respond to him. All she wanted to do was go to sleep, but the messages attached to this night prevented her from doing so. Lurking in the back of her mind, far from the light of awareness, was the belief that anything less than earth-shattering lovemaking indicated a flaw in their marriage. It never even occurred to her that she could decline to abide by this tradition. The cultural messages and the consequent beliefs were too strong.

Joanna had a similar experience. She and her husband had decided to wait until their wedding night to have intercourse. She thought they would have ripped each other's clothes because of the passion and anticipation that had been building over the last year and a half. But when they stood there after the wedding, they looked at each other and felt awkward. She said:

Our wedding night was hard. It was definitely not the blissful event that it is made out to be. As soon as we got back to the hotel room, I shut down. We just stood there like, "What are we supposed to do?" I wish I had communicated what I wanted, which was, "I'm exhausted and I just need to sleep." I was so tired. But I was afraid of hurting him, or that he would feel abandoned by me. Not to mention the whole myth about the wedding night!

Diana said that she was surprised that she and her husband made love on their wedding night despite her body's contrary yearnings: "It was unusual because we normally don't make love by rote, just because it's expected—on New Year's Eve or Valentine's Day." Her comment points to the fact that while women feel pushed to comply by this tradition because of the cultural messages, they may also be responding to the underlying meaning of the ritual. Diana felt that the act arose not from a culturally imposed fear but from a deeper impetus. Here the deeper impetus is the completion of a significant rite of incorporation. Making love on the wedding night is a ritual performed in many cultures around the world whose function is to bring the sacred act of marriage into the body and further consecrate lover and beloved unto each other. The act also signifies that bride and groom have transformed into husband and wife. In the past, most women and men were virgins when they married and the act of making love broke the seal of their singlehood and initiated them into the realm of a married couple. Today, although this is usually not the case, the act still carries the symbolic resonance of its underlying meaning. The bride has several rituals that symbolize her transformation of identity; this is one ritual that bride and groom share to acknowledge that their roles within the relationship have changed.

Despite the timeless meaning of this ritual, the fact that brides and grooms are usually not virgins on their wedding night changes the implications of the act. Ultimately the wedding night symbolizes the transformation from one state of being to another, and some women said that making love did not sufficiently symbolize the change. Lena, in contemplating her upcoming marriage, wanted to enact a physical ritual that would represent the psychological change within the relationship. She said:

My fiancé and I are far from virgins. In fact, we have both been married before. But on our wedding night, we want to enact a ritual that sanctifies our commitment of marriage, much the way the sexual act has always done. So we decided that in order to make this special and new, to acknowledge concretely that something had changed for us as a couple, we will have unprotected sex for the first time on our wedding night. We will welcome the possibility of creating new life. In a way I think this will make me feel like a virgin again, and it also embraces the notion that he and I are merging and letting each other in on an even deeper level.

Similarly, Joanna and Peter waited until their wedding night to have intercourse. Neither were virgins, but both felt that they wanted to wait until they were married to take their relationship to the next level. Anna also wanted an acknowledgment that she had changed as an individual and that her relationship to her husband had changed after the wedding. Although they had been together for five years and lived together for three, they both needed something new to symbolize the transformation of their union. She felt the wedding signified the birth of their marriage and she wanted to symbolize this new birth by moving into a fresh space together. She said:

We bought a house together shortly before we married and we decided that we wouldn't move in until after our wedding. To us, this symbolized the new life we were starting as husband and wife. I felt like we were not the same couple that we had always been. I especially felt different, like I had left some of my girlish nature behind and stepped fully into the role of woman. Buying and moving into a new house made this real. It was an external reality that confirmed what I was feeling inside. And when we moved into the house everything became us. It was as if our things—his books, my cookware, his stereo—had merged into our books, cookware, and stereo, just as getting married and the wedding had solidified our merging as a couple.

No matter how the bride and groom decide to symbolize the change, the wedding night represents the close of the wedding time and the beginning of the marriage. On this night, the transformation of identity that began for the woman many months earlier reaches an element of completion. At last she emerges, shocked, elated, and exhausted, from the white cocoon of her bridehood. Finally, she has become a wife.

Questions to Contemplate

🦋 What are you most excited about when you think of your wedding day?

🦋 What are you most nervous about when you think of your wedding day? What is your number-one fear?

🦋 How do you feel about getting married? Explore the positive feelings of excitement, joy, and anticipation, as well as the underbelly, the darker emotions, those feelings that our culture doesn't readily accept with regard to the wedding and the marriage.

🦋 The wedding day, like all rites of passage, is like a microcosm of life. It involves death and rebirth, decay and beauty, grief and joy. In this single, transformative day, all emotions tend to reveal themselves. How do you imagine yourself feeling on your wedding day?

🦋 How can you prepare for the possibility of an experience in which your emotions feel conflicting and paradoxical, quickly shifting from bliss to sadness, from absence to presence, from wilted to vibrant? Can you recall any experience in your past where you felt this duality of emotions?

🦋 Brides sometimes share feelings of regret concerning whom they chose to include in their wedding party. One bride included a sister-in-law with whom there was some animosity because she didn't want to cause a conflict. Another bride allowed her mother into the dressing room even though she always brought a well of anxiety with her. The women who surround you on your wedding day should create a sense of serenity. You will be in the midst of a profound transformation, in an extremely vulnerable state of being, and the members of your bridal party, your "attendants", are there to attend to you, to protect and nourish you.

Spend some time thinking about the women in your life. Who helps you to connect to your true nature? Who carries an air of serenity and peace about her and helps you to connect to those spaces in yourself? With whom do you feel tension? Imagine that you are like a newborn baby on your wedding day: pure skin, untouched and somewhat untouchable, in a heightened state of sensitivity. Who do you want to surround you in this space? Who do you not want around you?

🐾 How can your loved ones best support you on this day? After you have explored your wishes, you may want to share them with those around you.

🐾 Brides often share that they had difficulty being present on their wedding day. They felt as if they were floating, or not quite in their body. In the context of liminality, when a bride is between identities, this makes sense. Yet the way a bride wants to feel on that day often drastically differs from this model. What are your expectations for how you will feel on your wedding day? How will you attend to yourself if the reality differs from the expectation?

🐾 Similarly, brides often say that they felt too exhausted on their wedding night to make love, yet they complied out of fear of breaking tradition or because they had never considered that they could decline. What are your expectations of your wedding night? What are your fiancé's expectations? Have you discussed the issue with your fiancé? What are your beliefs or stories attached to not making love that night?

🐝 Think about rituals that symbolize your transition. What physical act represents the change and new birth that your relationship will undergo?

Chapter Six

The First Year

I've been looking at the women I know who are wives. I was at my bachelorette party and almost all of the women were married, a few had children, and I was looking at them thinking, "These are all great women." I feel like I can redefine what the word "wife" means to me.

—Helen

I have been conditioned to believe that honoring my own needs means losing my partner. I think part of this comes from the role model of my parents' relationship in which my mother dampened her fire to avoid losing my father's love and affection. My mother was a very independent person, a free spirit, and this threatened my father—he was afraid that her vitality and freedom meant that he would lose her. So she quieted her passions. This is what I saw, so it makes sense that I am afraid of this happening.

–Paulina

After I created this beautiful day that I spent months and months planning I felt like everyday was supposed to be like that. I don't think the traditional wedding acknowledges the daily reality of marriage. I think when you're getting married you need to know that there is no fairy tale. The fairy tale lies in the normal, everyday interactions. That's what marriage is about and that's what should be cherished. It's a daily process of getting married and wedding with each other every single day.

—Jade

Rites of Incorporation: Becoming a Wife

The process of becoming a wife defines the final phase of the wedding journey. The process evolves slowly, for just as a woman should not be expected to shed her singlehood identity in one day, so she cannot instantly transform into a wife the moment she steps out of her gown. In the first days of marriage, the woman may still be reeling from the wedding and the months that preceded her momentous event. It's common for a bride to feel bewildered, depressed, confused, and paralyzed by the varied emotional states that swirl within her during these first days or months. This state can be exacerbated if she hasn't allowed herself to feel any loss or fear during her engagement. It is important to remember that depression that affects the newly married woman is a normal, healthy response to the enormous change in her life. Her life has been irrevocably altered and it will take some time to adjust to her new status and reconcile the inner transformation that has occurred. The awareness that she can never return to the single lifestyle and that the person beside her will be there every day for the rest of her life is, for some women, a sobering realization that may not have hit home until after the wedding.

The task for the newly married woman is to pass through what van Gennep (1960) called *rites of incorporation*, specific ritual acts and shifts in consciousness that assist the process of incorporating her status as wife and merging with her husband in a new way. Ideally, she has separated from her family of origin and singlehood identity during the engagement; she has endured the uncomfortable transition in the liminal phase; and now she is prepared to focus her energy on the task of incorporation. When the first two phases, of separation and transition, are passed through with consciousness and guidance, the last phase can gracefully unfold. However, given that most of us are thrust into the role of wife without adequate psychological preparation, the soil from which the identity takes root is often dry and shaky. Unprepared for the enormity of the task, many women awaken on the first morning of marriage in a state of shock.

It is interesting to note that more has been written on the first year of marriage than on the engagement and wedding combined. Alarmed by research showing that 50.9% of couples nationwide will divorce in their first year, experts rush to provide cures for ailments that have escalated to a full-blown panic. This culture typically treats symptoms instead of rummaging beneath the surface to ferret out the causes. The woman who crumbles into an implacable depression or escapes into an affair during her first year of marriage is symptomatically indicating a failure to complete the rites of separation and transition at their appropriate times. In other words, she did not take the time to grieve her singlehood, let go of that way of life, realize the implications of entering into a lifetime commitment, discuss her fears about making this commitment, and allow herself to attend consciously to the emotions spawned by her engagement. When these ungrieved losses and fears surface in the first months, she thinks she has made a mistake and assumes her feelings of entrapment are caused by her marriage. It is more likely that she feels trapped by the mass of emotions that she has no idea how to manage. These emotions, coupled with unrealistic expectations about what marriage is supposed to provide, can hinder the incorporation process.

Jade was bewildered by the confusion that set in almost immediately following her wedding. She and her partner, Fernando, had been together for eight years before they married. She certainly felt that she knew him well and was ready to further their commitment through marriage. She was not prepared for the doubts and questions that troubled her for the first six months:

After the wedding, when my role as wife was established, there was a hesitation of, "Oops—did I really want to do this? Is he the right person? What have I just lost?" There was a freedom that was no longer present. It was confusing because I was also very happy. I had days of "What have I done?," other days of "I'm so happy I did this," and then other days of "I'm not sure how I feel about this." I still don't understand it. I've just written it off as one of my moods.

Her questioning, although scary, is not uncommon. It is unlikely that she made a mistake—Jade was one of the women in chapter 1 who said that she knew from the moment she met her husband that she would marry him, *and* they had had more than sufficient time together to confirm this initial knowing. It is more likely that her internal emotional state felt overwhelming, and she attributed this to the most obvious change in her life: the marriage. Yet it is not her marriage, her union with her husband, that is causing her to question, but the incomplete psychological transition that prefaced the marriage. Her questions indicate that she didn't let go of her singlehood enough to transition smoothly into wife. She described feeling a sense of loss. She longed for the freedom of "being a girlfriend, where you can always leave, to being a wife, where it is much more difficult to leave." It doesn't matter how long a couple has been together before they marry. A marriage is a rite of passage no matter when it occurs, and the woman must still pass through the phases of her transformation. She must die, she must sit in the unknown, and then she will be reborn.

Vivian also questioned her marriage in the early months. Her confusion began on their honeymoon:

I felt emotionally numb that first night. I remember waking up the next morning realizing that it was our first night as a married couple. We had sex and afterwards I felt numb and disappointed. He didn't feel like the love of my life. It wasn't the most passionate sex I had ever had. But then we had a great time on the honeymoon. I remember walking on the beach with him feeling very sure that this was my lifetime partner. I have to say, though, that the questioning came back off and on through the first year: "What have I done? I've made the worst mistake of my life." I remember two months into the marriage calling up a girlfriend on the other side of the country and saying, "I think I've made a terrible mistake. I think I'm going to have a shorter marriage than Dennis Rodman!" She said, "In a year I will ask you again. I felt the exact same way two months into my marriage." I think I had preconceived ideas of marriage, assuming that every day is going to be so happy, assuming that every day I was going to love everything about him. Some days I feel great and close to him but who knows how I'll feel tomorrow?

Just as our expectations of how the wedding itself should look interfere with the emotional process, our expectations of what marriage should look like interfere with the delicate task at hand of incorporating this person into the innermost layers of our lives. Where we should be negotiating what it means to be a wife, we are questioning if we even want to be a wife. Where we should be allowing the meaning of this commitment to settle into our consciousness, we are wondering if we should have made the commitment to begin with. Both Jade and Vivian struggled with the realization that a degree of their independence was sacrificed to the marriage. While some of these feelings are normal, when they cause the newlywed woman to question seriously whether or not she made the right decision it's likely she is dealing with the residue of unfinished rites of separation.

Even if the separations have been made within their appropriate time frame, women will often feel moments when their singlehood and daughter-identity pulse to the surface. Victoria, who entered her wedding with more preparation and consciousness than the average bride, experienced the final cutting of the cords to her family of origin six months after her wedding. She aptly likened the feeling to the cutting of her umbilical cord, and this comparison makes sense. After the baby is born and has endured the most painful separation, there is still one more cut that must be made. For Victoria, the cut occurred around Christmas plans. She had spent every single Christmas of her twenty-eight years with her family, but the Christmas after her wedding, her husband proposed that they travel abroad and spend it alone. As much as the romantic idea appealed to her, she resisted actually implementing it. She describes how she felt with a lightness that indicates her awareness of the deeper meaning:

This is when my umbilical cord is being cut and I don't want it! I don't want to go. I don't want to leave my family. I feel so sad for my poor little parents! And my poor grandma. My husband is ripping me away! I know that's not true, but that's how it feels. I feel ripped from my family. Going to the cabin like we've always done feels so safe and warm; Europe feels so cold and far away. This feels so painful.

Victoria did take the trip with her husband. She knew that it was the right decision, that it was an important step in establishing her new family. Inherent in the task of incorporation is the transfer of allegiance; this helps solidify the new partnership. As Victoria realized, it wasn't a matter of choosing between her husband and her family of origin, but rather of seeing that her husband *is* her family now and she must choose which family will assume priority over the holidays. With the wedding, woman and man do become family. The spiritual transformation that happens during the ceremony binds the bride and groom in a way that defies tangible reality. As Vivian said, "All of a sudden I'm thick as blood."

It doesn't matter if the bride and groom are in their twenties or their forties, if they have been together for ten years or ten months—the change of identity elicited by marriage is profound. Rites of incorporation are about coming to terms with these changes, beginning to understand what the role of wife means to each woman and what the role of husband means to each man, and beginning the lifelong challenge of maintaining an alive, honest, and fulfilling marriage. It is easy to think of the wedding as an ending, the final celebration after a year of concentrated planning, and the culmination of a lifelong search for one's true partner. Culturally, this belief has been imprinted into our subconscious—how many films, novels, plays, and television shows *end* when the couple finally marry? While in many ways the wedding is an ending, it is also a beginning. It is the ending of the lives of two single people and the beginning of the marriage. Both bride and groom have been changed as individuals and as a couple. Like all changes, it takes some getting used to.

The Wedding Lasts a Day— the Marriage, a Lifetime

The first change the woman must adjust to is no longer being a bride. Sometimes the act of incorporating the new roles of wife and husband cannot even begin until the woman comes to terms with the deflation that naturally occurs after the wedding. For the past several months, the woman has been almost exclusively focused on this single event. As we have seen, even women who never thought they would become "that bride" found themselves awakened at dawn by thoughts of their wedding. Work, friends, and even her fiancé often took a back seat to the wedding planning throughout the engagement. As much as she experienced grief or anxiety in the months preceding the wedding, she still looked forward to her day with utmost anticipation. If she is a woman who dreamed about her wedding day from the time she was a little girl—imagining her gown, the guests, her fiancé waiting for her at the altar—the anticipation would have been especially high. There are few days in life that we look forward to with as much excitement, expectation, and energy as the wedding day. When a woman begins planning her wedding, her focus turns upward and forward, singlemindedly channeling her attention toward creating a beautiful, unearthly day.

And then the day happens. It comes and it goes and it lasts only as long as a single day can possibly last. The newly married woman awakens the next day and realizes that it's all over. The day that *will be* is the day that *was*. What happens to all that energy and focus? What does she have to look forward to now? With the realization that she is no longer a bride and that her wedding day is over, she experiences the first faint tinges of the post-wedding blues. Carmen felt the depression set in when the guests were leaving the reception:

I felt so sad when everyone was leaving. Everyone flying out, going back to their homes and countries. Weddings should last a week. The next day was a real letdown. I felt depressed and down, realizing that it was all over. I didn't think it would hit me the way it did. Before the wedding, everything was about getting married—"I can't get together because I'm getting married" or "I can't take on extra work because I'm getting married." Everything was leading to this day. Now there's nothing to plan for. It's a downer.

It is, in fact, just that: a downer. For what comes up must come down, and it naturally follows that all the hype about the wedding would be followed by a deflation. This experience of transitional depression, which often follows Christmas, a new job, a large artistic performance, or any other event toward which a lot of energy has been directed, is described by what psychologists call *social displacement theory*. This theory posits that what is initially experienced as elation and optimism is followed by frustration, depression, and confusion as the reality of the adjustment required by one's new life sets in. In other words, the fairy tale of the wedding day is over, and the reality of marriage begins. We live in a culture that does little to prepare us for the reality of marriage. Even if we intellectually realize that marriage is not a fairy tale, we still carry the impression that somehow things should be misty and light after the wedding day. We got married, we wore the white dress, we walked down the aisle, we cut the cake, and now we are supposed to live "happily ever after." But when happily ever after turns into day after regular day of eating breakfast, going to work, and meeting this man at the dinner table or in bed, our illusion is pierced. Jade talked about how the wedding illusion affected her new marriage:

After I created this beautiful day that I spent months and months planning I felt like everyday was supposed to be like that. I don't think the traditional wedding acknowledges the daily reality of marriage. I think when you're getting married you need to know that there is no fairy tale. The fairy tale lies in the normal, everyday interactions. That's what marriage is about and that's what should be cherished. It's a daily process of getting married and wedding with each other every single day. I think the wedding, in our culture, sets up illusions from the get-go.

Jade quickly realized that, although she and her husband felt changed by the wedding, the wedding itself didn't magically change them. In one sense, the entire bridal experience *is* suffused with an elusive and unearthly innocence and perfection. There are moments on the wedding day that transcend the human realm, moments where we are transported to a place of light and purity. But, as these women realized, these are just moments, and if we cling to them as a conception of what must exist on a daily basis in the marriage, we are setting ourselves up for vast disappointment. What we can do is hold those transcendent, divine moments as reminders of our highest selves, as individuals and as a couple. In the days, weeks, or months following the wedding the woman must come back down to earth, stepping out of her beautiful bridal gown and becoming human again. Deflation naturally ensues as she adjusts to normal life.

Postbridal Depression: Another Wedding Shadow

For some women, the postwedding blues was the extent of their depression. After they adjusted to no longer being a bride, they bounced back into their regular rhythm and resumed their lives. For most, however, the profound change of the wedding is met with not just the blues, but a subtle depression. The word depression still carries negative connotations in this culture, although this has begun to change. Depression is often regarded with embarrassment or condescension, and it's rarely discussed outside of "appropriate" settings like therapists' offices and mental institutions. Contrary to popular understanding, depression can manifest in a variety of forms, such as loss of self-esteem, loss of perspective, sadness, difficulty eating and sleeping, fatigue or loss of energy, irritability, fearfulness, psychosomatic complaints, and a desire to avoid being with people. Far from being dysfunctional and cause for shame, depression is actually the body's healthy response to profound change. Psychologist F.F. Flach (1974) described it this way: "Change of any kind, if it touches something or someone of importance to the individual, is usually met with depression. The process of growing up and growing older involves a series of changes; every transitional phase of life, from childhood to marriage to old age, requires some degree of giving up, of letting go. In order to move successfully from one phase to the next, a person must be able to experience depression in a direct and meaningful way" (31).

Leah Heidenrich, in her Master's thesis entitled *Bride Illusion: Depression in Newlywed Women* (1990), found that every woman she interviewed experienced some form of depression in her first year of marriage. While some newlyweds did experience depression in an extreme form, most women carried on with their normal lives but felt displaced or like their inner spark had been temporarily quelled. The most common manifestations of the depression were sadness, anxiety, fatigue, and anger. In a culture that pathologizes depression, viewing it as something that should be ignored or overcome, guilt often accompanies these emotions. Heidenrich wrote: "A wedding and a new marriage "shouldn't" bring on depression. Our romantic picture portrays this time in our life as idyllic and romantic. Women's guilt around their unacceptable feelings of depression manifests itself as psychosomatic ailments, anger, and negative projections onto the husband and onto the relationship" (68).

Far from being something that should be cast aside, depression is often a necessary response to any rite of passage. When we pass from one status, or way of life, to another, we commonly sink into a quiet solitude in honor of the transition. "Sinking into" an experience is a deeply feminine way of moving through emotions. Through complete acceptance of *what is*, the emotion is transformed and a higher state is revealed. Men (or those more identified with their masculine nature) tend to swashbuckle their way through the vines and tumbleweeds of their emotional terrain. The contrasting methods of moving through transition are poignantly acted out in the first months of marriage. While the wedding transition touches both partners, each may seize the quest in different ways. As Johnson wrote: "When a woman is touched by an archetypal experience, she often collapses before it. It is in this collapse that she quickly recovers her archetypal connection and restores her inner being . . . A woman does this in a different way than a man. While he probably has to go out seeking a heroic task and kill many dragons and rescue fair maidens, she generally has to withdraw to a very quiet place and remain still" (47).

Joanna unwittingly described her first months of marriage as if they were specifically patterned along these archetypal lines:

Those first months were so hard. It felt like hell. First of all, we coped very differently with transition. I would get very lethargic. I wasn't working at all, I was in a career transition, and I could barely get out of bed. And Peter had just opened his new vocal studio so he went the other extreme of go go go go go, do do do. So here he was going a hundred miles an hour and there I was like a snail, barely able to move. And he's looking at me saying, "Is she ever going to get a job or unpack some of these boxes while I'm gone?" And I'm looking at him saying, "Why is he so stressed out? Who is this person?"

Joanna intuitively retreated to a place where healing could occur; her husband intuitively charged into battle to manage the transition. Each coping mechanism serves a function and neither should be criticized. It might be helpful for newlyweds to understand how polarized they can become when confronted with a profound, archetypal experience. With understanding comes acceptance, and with acceptance arises the possibility of moving through the darkness and meeting one another on the other side.

Diana's experience of depression had a cocoonlike quality to it. She felt removed from the world as she sank into many hours of quiet reflection, marked by bouts of crying and an acute sense that she and her husband had been affected quite differently by the marriage. She said:

After my wedding I fell into the deepest depression I have ever experienced. I would move from room to room and sit on the edges of pieces of furniture. Sometimes hours would go by and I think I didn't blink. I had no idea what I was feeling, but it sent me back into therapy. It was when I started real therapy. I would go to my therapist and sit and look at her and cry. I couldn't say anything. For weeks I went up to her like that, and at a hundred dollars an hour, mind you! I would just sit there. I had no idea what had happened to me. I kept thinking, "It doesn't make sense to have these feelings in relation to the event."

When Diana explored what had happened to her, she realized that her perfectionistic attention to the details of her wedding was a defense against grieving the losses beforehand. All of the loss that she had pushed aside before the wedding came tumbling through her after the event. She was also adjusting to her new role as wife and grieving the loss of her single status:

I was thirty-eight when I married and I never thought of myself as a maiden, but what I did feel was that I was my own person, that I belonged to myself. I had married a prominent doctor in a small community and all of a sudden I was not Diana anymore but "the wife." I felt like my husband was magnified by the marriage—now he was a doctor with a wife and a nice home—and I was somehow simplified.

In the context of rites of passage, in which there is always a symbolic death, a transition time, and a rebirth, depression makes sense. But in our modern view of weddings, which says that these first months are supposed to be among the most alive, passionate, and joyous times of one's life, depression has no place. If depression is denied or forced underground, it will warp into another emotion. As Heidenrich pointed out, guilt-laden depression often manifests as anger toward the husband or regrets about the marriage. Because of the cultural expectations and a lack of accurate information on transition, these first few months are often confusing for newlyweds. Instead of understanding that the depression is normal and necessary, they misinterpret its presence as an indication that something is wrong with the marriage. Much of the pressure is relieved when we can name our experience and understand its purpose.

What Is a Wife?

As the depression runs its course and the woman's spark returns, she begins the process of becoming a wife. What does it mean to become a wife today? In the months immediately preceding and following the wedding, this question often roams through womens' minds. When our grandmothers married, the answer was obvious. She would do what her mother did, and her grandmother before her, and her great-grandmother before that. For as far back through the long line of her family as anyone could recall, to be a wife was to care for one's husband, to bear children, to cook, nurture, and support, and to tend to the garden of one's family, all so that everyone would be healthy, well loved, and well nourished. A wife's work was in her home, while her husband went into the world and provided the economic support. The roles, although restrictive and confining, were clearly defined.

With our mothers' generation, the roles began to loosen. Many of us grew up with mothers, single or married, who worked outside the home and provided equal financial contribution to the family. These mothers may or may not have cooked dinner in the evening, picked us up from school, or worked in the garden, but they provided strong role models as women who achieved independence and manifested their dreams.

With our mothers and our grandmothers as our immediate role models, not to mention the plethora of possibilities for women we see depicted in the media, we often feel stretched across the two poles of seemingly contradictory options for wifedom. Is a wife someone whose primary occupation is caring for her husband and her children, cooking delicious meals, keeping the house clean, and always being available as a source of emotional support? Or is a wife the equal partner of her husband, the two contributing as equally to finances as to the maintenance of the home and the emotional sustenance of the marriage?

Helen was surprised by her negative reaction to the word wife and the images that stepping into that role conjured up for her. She married at age thirty-two and had spent the previous ten years supporting herself through a successful career in the business world. She had enjoyed her independent lifestyle in downtown Chicago but was prepared to relinquish aspects of her freedom when she entered marriage. A month before her wedding she felt stumped by how to make the transition into being a wife. What does that mean? Who and what would she become? While she felt extremely positive about spending the rest of her life with Andrew, she was surprised when she came up against "a wall of a negative identity" of herself as a wife. To confuse matters, she quit her job two months before the wedding to create time to pursue an independent business. Being unemployed for the first time in years brought on worries that she would be suctioned into the dependent wife role and "become this drag on the system." She also noticed that a part of her wanted to take care of Andrew and felt confused about what that meant:

I feel a sense of responsibility that I have never felt, and that leads me into the Martha Stewart/Stepford wives ideas about what it means to be a "good" wife. All of a sudden I'm thinking I have to keep the house clean and have dinner on the table. And I don't even know where this is coming from. Our lives are not structured that way at all—we go out to dinner almost every night, or we have something brought in. I haven't cooked since I've lived in Chicago! And then we talk about having kids and what comes up in that context is, "Am I really going to raise my kids on take-out?" I just have no idea who I'm going to be as a wife. And part of it is the surprise of where these voices are coming from. It suggests such a backward way: Okay, you're a wife now, so this is the template that you have to follow.

When she took the time to explore where these voices were coming from, she traced them back to her own grandmothers and mother. Both of her grandmothers had followed the traditional model of wife as nurturer and homemaker; her mother had also followed this model until her divorce forced her to join the work world. Helen knew that she never wanted to be dependent on a man financially, but she didn't know what role her traditional wife instincts would play in the marriage.

While Helen felt a general societal message and the patterns of her personal history pressuring her to be a certain kind of wife, Carmen felt the pressure from her groom. She realized a few months before her wedding that her impending marriage brought some of the underlying issues in her relationship into focus. When they would argue about the same things they had always argued about in their five years together, her groom would respond with, "Is this going to happen when we get married?" She said:

I think my fiancé thinks that once we get married, I'm going to be the perfect wife and I am not going to make the same mistakes that I make now, like: I'm going to wash the dishes right away and I'm going to clean the house and I'm going to vacuum and do the laundry. I'm sure he's imagining me in a little apron in a spotless house once we get married! I think he's expecting a miraculous transformation to occur and I feel that pressure. I tell him that it's not realistic to expect that. I may be more responsible but I can't see myself changing much in any way. And I don't expect him to change either.

Each woman must discover for herself what it means to be a wife. We don't have a template to follow, and yet because of our thousands of years of modeling (and our instinctually feminine nature), we find ourselves led to behave in traditional wife ways. Part of the postwedding transition is about discovering who we are within this new role. It's not like we can flick a switch and have a new identity. These first months, or years, are a time to test out different ways of being in the marriage and slowly develop into the wife you want to be. We are at a unique time in history where women can choose what role they want to assume in the marriage. Some women may want to stay at home and raise the children. Others may want to participate as equal partners with their husband in every realm. There is no correct way to be a wife. It is up to us, women of the millennium, to define the role, and the word, anew.

Many women attached negative connotations to the word itself and refused to refer to themselves as "wife." When Helen's sister got married, she felt so uncomfortable with the word wife that she preferred to refer to herself as her husband's mistress! She thought the word mistress was sexier and more fun whereas wife sounded dowdy and boring. Dana said that the word wife sounded like "A German milkmaid out milking cows with pink cheeks." She couldn't find another suitable word, however: "Partner sounds dry; lover sounds smarmy; spouse sounds too old-fashioned. There is no good language for it."

Perhaps as the role of wife evolves and expands so will the connotation of the word itself. In response to her negative impressions Helen decided to create a collage from magazines and photos that depicted the kind of wife she wanted to be. As she became aware of her associations, she realized that she could change the direction of that thinking and create new, concrete images of what being a wife meant to her:

I've also been looking at the women I know who are wives. I was at my bachelorette party and almost all of the women were married, a few had children, and I was looking at them thinking, "These are all great women." I feel like I can redefine what that word means to me.

Helen realized that she had been resisting a natural impulse to cook for her husband and nurture him in tangible ways. She saw that she had been attaching meaning and implications to these acts—"If I cook for him that means I will never work and I will become dependent"—instead of seeing them as beautiful expressions of her love for him. It is important to ask ourselves honest questions when these impulses arise: Are they originating from deeply ingrained cultural messages that tell us that we have to do certain things to be a good wife, or are they springing from a healthy desire to nurture and take care of the people we love? Neither denying a natural impulse nor blindly falling into a predetermined role will aid us in our progress toward becoming the wife we want to be. As Sara said,

After we got married, I suddenly found myself wanting to make blueberry muffins for my husband! I felt happily possessed by this idea of him coming home from work to a fresh tray of steaming muffins. But that didn't mean that I was submissive and dependent. I still had my career aspirations. I just felt like making him some muffins! My friends laughed at me. It was such a stereotype of "the wife." Honestly, I find things like cooking and gardening, even folding laundry, quite meditative, and I resent that those tasks have been associated with the idea that I am demeaning myself for my husband. Do I want to be his maid? No. Do I want to excel in my career? Absolutely. I think balance is possible. I think it's possible for both sexes.

Many women today are trying to achieve a balance between domesticity and career, nurturer and achiever, being and doing, feminine and masculine. They also realize that the challenge of blending the beauty of both extremes into one role cannot be resolved in the first months of marriage. As we are on the threshold of a new frontier regarding sex roles, the role models for women who have achieved this balance are limited. Without many role models or a traditional template to follow, it may take several years before we feel comfortable with the role of wife we have chosen. When we enter marriage, we are handed a clean canvas entitled "Wife." It is up to us to fill in the colors and images, to paint the landscapes of the wife we want to be.

The "I" Within the "We"

One of the most challenging tasks of incorporating, or being truly *married*, is figuring out how to maintain our individuality within the marriage. Questions emerge during the first months of marriage that reflect the increased level of merging within the relationship: Can I blossom as an individual within the union of marriage? If I reach toward my potential, will my husband feel threatened and withdraw his love from me? If I stifle aspects of myself, will I feel suffocated and grow to resent my husband and my marriage? These questions may have surfaced before the wedding, but the total union with another that the wedding solidifies often elicits the most primal fears. The art of achieving interdependence—of embracing the full powers of oneself while merging with another—is a lifelong challenge. But in the first months of marriage, after she has surrendered so much of herself through the wedding process, the newlywed woman often finds this challenge dominating her consciousness.

Paulina felt that her individual self had become lost during the early years of her relationship with Ryan. The loss of self felt intolerable after the wedding and in her first months of marriage she tried desperately to retrieve her "I" from her husband's embrace. She wrote constantly about the challenge, sensing that unless she addressed it directly in these early years, she would lose herself completely and, consequently, lose the vitality of the marriage. She found, like many women, that our culture doesn't support people, especially women, taking care of themselves within marriage. She became aware of the legacy of codependence in which one partner silences their true needs to avoid a conflict. These patterns of behavior had been handed down for generations; like the role-modeling of wifedom, it is often the cultural inheritance of women. Here she shares the beginning of her exploration on how to maintain the "I" within the "we." Two months after her wedding, she wrote:

I am trying to find myself again within this relationship. I got lost somewhere along the way and now I have to take tiny steps, tiny acts that honor my voice and my needs. Like today while we were walking: We automatically grasped hands, but in that moment I did not want to hold hands. I wanted my arms free to swing at my own pace and according to the rhythms of my own body, so I let go. He took my hand again, and again I let go. Finally I said, "I don't feel like holding hands right now." I was afraid that he would be angry, but he wasn't. He was fine.

During the first year of her relationship with Ryan, long before they married, they had forged a single road from the two separate paths of their individual selves. As normally occurs in the first months or years of a relationship, they had wanted to unite in every way possible. If Ryan went to the market, Paulina was sure to join him. If Paulina went for a bike ride, Ryan wanted to come along. They wanted to share food, chairs, clothes, and anything else that would weave their two essences into a symbiotic relationship.

This joining is a healthy part of the beginning of a relationship in which the bond between the couple is solidified. When two people fall in love, they become enraptured in the silky threads of a single nest and enchanted by the magical world that is exclusively theirs. Eventually, however, when the threads begin to feel more gluey than silky and their world feels more constricting than enchanting, they each, in their own way, start to separate from the relationship. But when Paulina tried to separate out, she realized that she was battling the parental role models and societal messages that expressed how to be a good wife. In her fourth month of marriage she wrote:

I have been conditioned to believe that honoring my own needs means losing my partner. I think part of this comes from the role model of my parents' relationship in which my mother dampened her fire to avoid losing my father's love and affection. My mother was a very independent person, a free spirit, and this threatened my father—he was afraid that her vitality and freedom meant that he would lose her. So she quieted her passions. This is what I saw, so it makes sense that I am afraid of this happening.

I also think I am responding to a general societal message: Women are supposed to sacrifice their needs for their men, to place the man first, and to squelch their vitality because it is "too much" or too threatening. Because we sacrifice and squelch and succumb, I see women as equally responsible for these dynamics. The messages are deeply ingrained into both sexes. When I understand where I come from, it helps me to understand how I am. Now I can focus on how I want to be.

Eventually—after she let go of his hand and stopped cooking and cleaning out of obligation and went away for the weekend with a girlfriend and listened to her inner "no" even when Ryan enticed her toward "yes"—Paulina discovered that her husband didn't withdraw his love and affection when she expressed her needs or separated from him. In fact, to her delight and surprise, once she began to take steps in these directions Ryan encouraged her to continue. This is not to say that the challenge of their interdependence was immediately resolved. Rather, she learned that it was never her husband who impeded her self-growth, but herself. Now, four years after her wedding, she says that she still finds this topic a challenge. Although their movement in and out of togetherness and separateness is more fluid, she feels that the challenge of each nourishing their individual selves within an intimate marriage will continue for the rest of their lives.

As women on a new frontier, we will likely struggle with the voices of our childhood and our culture with regard to this issue. We will also struggle with fears that try to stomp out our needs and desires. And we will find that it takes effort, consciousness, and a daily commitment to maintain the "I" within the "we." But the effort is certainly worth it. Deep down we instinctually know that a marriage cannot remain alive and passionate if one or both partners is asleep. Marriage, while certainly creating a spiritual merging, doesn't literally combine two into one. Each partner is still an individual person, complete with their needs, dreams, longings, and feelings, and it is each partner's responsibility to make sure that each of these areas within themselves is thoroughly attended to. As Jade wisely asserted:

I feel like since I've been married, my identity as an individual has been deleted. I am now Fernando and Jade, not just Jade. Fernando and I are saying no, we have a bond and a committed relationship but we are individuals, but socially the message is that we are one unit now. And if we buy into that we're going to be unhappy. I think what has made us last this long is that we glorify each other's spirit and give each other the respect of having a separate identity. If we stop doing that because we are married now, the relationship will fizzle out.

The One-Year Anniversary

The one-year anniversary is the final rite of incorporation that closes the circle of the wedding journey. Through the wedding, both partners took an enormous leap forward in their relationship, and it often takes at least a year to integrate these changes. As we have seen, the woman passes through a series of stages of incorporation—postwedding blues, postbridal depression, figuring out what it means to be a wife, learning how to be intimate with her husband without losing her self—and as she nears the end of this first year, she usually begins to feel comfortable with the integration of her new identity and her merging with her husband. The new level of incorporation is sometimes reflected in an increased comfort with the new last name. Jane, married over twenty-five years, said that by the end of her first year of marriage she finally felt comfortable saying her married name: "Before that I still felt strange, like I was saying that I was someone else." The new name, like the new identity, now falls easily off the tongue, representing that the woman's new skin as wife has finally taken hold. Emily knew that her transformation of identity was nearing completion when she felt comfortable referring to herself as "his wife" and to Mark as "her husband." "When we first got married and we used those terms, I felt like we were children playing house. There are times when it still sounds awkward to me, but overall it feels natural, like this is who we are." For Sophia, the completion of the wedding journey appeared in her dreams and was represented by her wedding gown:

Just before our one-year anniversary I started having dreams of a second wedding, which was calmer, smaller, and more intimate. In one dream I decided to take my wedding dress out of its vacuum-sealed box and wear it again. This gave me great pleasure. I felt like the princess part of me that I inhabited before and on my wedding day was a part of me again.

A subtext of the process of incorporation during this first year is that the woman often reintegrates the maiden aspect of herself that was "sacrificed" on the wedding day. Sophia felt that the two aspects of herself—maiden and wife—had been merged into a healthy whole. It was as if she had to relinquish that part of herself before merging with her husband, but now that the union was solidified, the maiden could reenter. Isabel, who deeply mourned the loss of her maidenhood the night before her wedding, shared Sophia's experience. She felt she had to completely let go of that aspect of herself, only to welcome the essence of maidenhood back into her inner world a year after the wedding:

Now I realize that I am a free, independent, childlike spirit as well as an interdependent wife. Both of these aspects of myself are present, and both are united with my soul mate. For a while I thought that I had to completely surrender certain aspects, like my independence, for the marriage. Now I've seen that I don't have to do that at all. But I think it took me at least a year of personal growth to realize that. I needed to let go and mourn an aspect of me before I could come back around into my full power.

These levels of incorporation, and the close of the wedding journey, are materially symbolized by the eating of the cake. Tradition instructs the bride and groom to freeze the top layer of their wedding cake so that it can be eaten on their one-year anniversary. The ritual of eating, as mentioned earlier, is a primary rite of incorporation. Partaking of a bread that was baked a year before is a way to bring the year into the body, come full circle, and complete a process that began with the engagement. Women added to the cake tradition and found their own, personalized ways of symbolizing this closure. Clare took her wedding dress out of its place in storage and ordered take-out from her and Shawn's favorite restaurant. They read their vows to each other, and dined on their living room floor dressed as bride and groom. "In a way it was the wedding that I wanted to have, just the two of us, and after this ritual I felt more complete about my wedding day." Sophia, together with her husband, bought a third ring to wear on her right hand. She felt that this third, "one-year anniversary ring" completed the trinity of her engagement and wedding rings. "Each ring symbolizes an aspect of myself and an element of my marriage with Mikael. No single ring is complete without the other two." Eve, like Clare, also created a ritual from the wedding dress. She had fallen in love with her dress the moment she saw it, but after the wedding, realizing that the dress represented the aspect of herself that she was sacrificing, she couldn't bear to look at it:

After the wedding I disregarded my dress. I never got it cleaned. I never put it away. For many months it hung in its plastic in the closet of my office, just sort of draped over cabinets. I saw it every single day but I wouldn't lift the plastic. As our one-year anniversary approached, I remembered that before we married I had all these ideas about cutting the dress and wearing it every anniversary.

So I finally lifted the plastic and took it from its morgue,
had it cleaned and cut, and wore it to dinner and
dancing.

The one-year anniversary is a milestone on the wedding
journey. It is around this time that women begin to integrate
the larger life lessons they learned through the wedding
experience. The passage of a full year offers the perspective
necessary to look back and make sense of what exactly happened through this process. It took a year for Sophia to
come to terms with the fact her wedding was less than perfect, but the lessons she learned from the experience were
invaluable:

I learned, really learned in my body, that life is now.
Because of how much energy I put into the wedding and
how disappointed I was by so many aspects of it, I am
now wary of looking forward to future events. This may
sound cynical but it actually feels liberating in that it
keeps me more in the moment. Someone once said to me,
"Expectation is the root of all suffering," and after my
wedding I understood that phrase. I am more wary of the
illusions that our culture holds out as panaceas to life's
problems—the messages in our culture that keep us
reaching for the next thing to bring us happiness—that
perfect boyfriend, that perfect wedding, then the house,
the children, the car, the better job. Those things may be
nice but they do not, in themselves, create happiness, and
it was my wedding that drove this point home for me. It
was a beautiful day and I do feel that the ceremony
served its purpose, but it was only a day, and there is
only so much that a single day can offer. I feel more
realistic around big days now—like New Year's and
birthdays—like in not having such grand expectations, I'm

actually able to enjoy whatever those days bring. It feels like a very important life lesson.

Isabel, Vivian, and Diana also learned important life lessons. After their weddings they all felt more firmly committed to listening to their own needs in the face of others' opinions. They all sacrificed too much of themselves around the wedding to please mothers, guests, society's ideal of perfection, or girlfriends. "I bent over backwards to make sure everyone's needs were attended to at the expense of enjoying my own wedding," Diana said. Like all lessons in life, the learning happens in layers. Because of the all-encompassing nature of the wedding, the learning that is inspired through this event sinks into several layers of the woman's psyche. The paradox is in wishing we could have learned these lessons before the wedding yet knowing that it was only through the wedding that we could have learned them. The beauty is in realizing that we can apply these lessons to every rite of passage in our lives, from the birth of a child, to moving, a job change, midlife, menopause, and old age. The lessons we learn through the wedding will inevitably reappear throughout our lives. Core issues unique to each individual are illuminated during rites of passage. So whether we are struggling with perfectionism, confronting our codependence, living for an illusory ideal, or learning how to feel our difficult feelings, the wedding shows us where we are with regard to these issues and offers an accelerated course in healing them. If we elect to take this course and study our internal texts, we will enter each future transition with more awareness, continually spiraling into deeper layers of ourselves and entering each new spiral with greater serenity.

Finally, the one-year anniversary is a seal on the wedding quest. It completes the wedding rites of incorporation that began during the ceremony and continued in increments through the first year of marriage. These rites included both the intrapersonal ways in which the woman integrated her new identity of wife as well as the interpersonal ways she merged with her husband. Of course these lessons don't end with the one-year anniversary. Rather, around this time the *wedding archetype* abates and the *marriage archetype* assumes priority. A woman may look back on the wedding with a certain nostalgia; she may stare wistfully at wedding gowns when she passes bridal stores. But she knows now that her time as bride has passed and she recognizes that her energy must now be channeled toward her most intimate relationship. The wedding she now focuses on is the daily wedding between wife and husband. The rites of incorporation that ask for her attention are those that increasingly close the gap between her and her husband. For although the wedding has come to a close, wife and husband are wedded every day. Through their union they discover, moment by moment, what it means to be married ... "for as long as you both shall live."

Questions to Contemplate

🐿 What does the term "marriage" mean to you? What are the most significant differences for you between being married and not being married?

🐿 How can you prepare for the letdown that usually follows the high of the wedding? How do you see the post-wedding blues affecting you?

🐿 What does the term "wife" mean to you? What have your role models for wives been? If the word has a negative connotation for you, what are some ways that you can redefine the word in a positive way?

🐿 When you think of the actions involved in being a wife, are these behaviors internally derived or externally imposed? In other words, do they stem from genuine desires and impulses or are they things you think you "should" do to be a good wife?

🐿 What does the term "husband" mean to you? Are you aware of any expectations you have when your identities change to "husband and wife"?

🐿 Getting married often changes a relationship. When a wedding achieves its purpose, which is to spiritually wed two separate individuals, the relationship is transformed. Two common issues that surface when a lifetime commitment is made are the fear of engulfment, which involves losing your identity, individuality, and freedom and the fear of abandonment and betrayal, which involves losing your partner to emotional withdrawal, divorce, death, or infidelity. How do you see your relationship changing after you marry? What are your core fears?

🐦 What is, or was, your parents' marriage like? What aspects do you hope to include in your own marriage? What aspects do you wish to avoid? What is, or was, your fiancé's parents' marriage like? Do you see any aspects of these marriages appearing in your relationship already?

🐦 Do you have any role models of healthy, vital, long-term marriages? What does a healthy marriage mean to you?

🐦 Our culture offers one ritual to symbolize the completion of the wedding journey: eating the top layer of the wedding cake on your first anniversary. What are some other ways you can concretely acknowledge this closure?

🐦 What lessons did you learn about yourself through the wedding journey? How do you see these lessons helping you transition more smoothly through future rites of passage? How will these lessons help you in your marriage?

🐦 How do you see you and your husband in . . . five years, ten years, twenty-five years, fifty years?

Chapter Seven

A New Vision of Marriage

Be aware that marriage will bring up some of the toughest issues you'll ever have to look at, and that that's a gift, not a burden or something to be avoided. Recognize that conflict is a blessing in disguise, and that it is through resolution of conflict that peace comes. And the greater the conflict, the greater the peace and joy. Be compassionate with yourself and your partner. Recognize that marriage is the most sacred and complex of all interpersonal relationships.

—Brian

About four years into my marriage I realized that I had been carrying resentment toward Sophia because she was failing to meet my expectations of what a "good" wife was. A good wife was supposed to be a gracious hostess, provide a loving, harmonious, peaceful home environment, be cordial and courteous to my work associates, offer sound business advice, welcome me when I came home from work with a kiss and a hot meal and, on top of all that, provide an exciting sex life! I can see now how backwards that list is, but it was the list that I carried into the marriage without even realizing it. A lot has changed since I have begun to let go of these expectations and realize that ultimately I need to provide many of those things for myself. I am learning what it means to really love Sophia and not some idea of what a wife is supposed to be.

—Mikael

Loving Brian is an expression of who I am. I believe that marriage is designed to require the very deepest in us, and to require complete commitment and devotion. It is also designed to give the greatest joy that we can have in this life.

—Beth

A Guiding Vision

This book has focused on the challenges, questions, and joys of the wedding process. But as challenging and joyous as *getting* married may be, the challenges and joys of actually *being* married are infinitely greater. And when the intense focus on the wedding dies down, we begin to ask ourselves many important questions about marriage: What does it mean to have a good marriage? How can we avoid falling into the high percentage of couples who divorce? How can we maintain the passion and vitality that initially attracted us to each other?

There are no easy answers to these questions. There are countless books on the subject of maintaining an alive, healthy marriage, each offering their own prescription for working with one of the most intricate of human relationships. The truth is that we are on the threshold of a new frontier regarding relations between the sexes. Never before, or not in recent history, have women and men been regarded as equals and the sex roles been so blurred. Just as we struggle with what it means to be a wife, so we must wrestle within ourselves for the answers to what it means to be married. In the past men and women entered marriage with a clear set of expectations about what their partner should provide and fulfill. Men were expected to "bring home the bacon" and women were expected to create a loving, harmonious home and family; men were the providers and women were the nourishers; men provided financially and women fulfilled the emotional needs of everyone in the family. The primary question in determining a suitable marriage partner was: How is this person going to complete me and meet my needs? The needs were clearly delineated and the primary task was to find someone who would skillfully and peacefully fulfill these needs.

For some couples, this traditional model may still work. Some men are content going out into the world and serving as the primary financial provider and some women are content in their role as homemaker. However, as women seek to further their development in the outer world and men seek to further their growth through developing a relationship to their inner, emotional world, the old model ceases to work. Women and men have been expanding their capacity for self-growth for the past thirty years. We are pushing the boundaries of the ways we have always functioned in the world, within ourselves, and with each other, and this monumental change necessitates monumental shifts in the model of marriage.

Women and men are becoming more balanced and self-contained as individuals. As women develop a relationship to their masculine side through meaningful work in the world, and men learn to relate internally to their feminine nature through feeling their feelings and becoming their own nurturers, we find ourselves gaining independence and no longer needing each other in the survivalistic ways we once did. Gary Zukav refers to this shift as becoming "the new man" and "the new woman." He suggests that each sex is striving for internal completion and that it is no longer fulfilling to look to our partner to complete us. If we do not seek each other to fulfill missing pieces in ourselves, what is the glue that holds us together? What are the new binding principles of marriage?

It is important to have a viable vision to support us through the rough patches that inevitably arise in marriage. When the vision of "you provide and I'll nourish" collapses, what is there to replace it? Several cutting-edge thinkers in the psychological world—including Zukav, John Welwood, and Kathlyn and Gay Hendricks—believe that the purpose of marriage has shifted from a model that supports dependence on one another to one that encourages interdependence. They espouse the concept that we are brought together to grow as individuals, and that one of the great challenges of the marriage path is to be willing to look within ourselves, as opposed to our partners, for the source of our problems. Welwood, in *Love and Awakening* (1996), offers: "Of course, facing the challenges of this path takes great courage and daring. This is where a guiding vision becomes essential: It helps two partners take heart and gather their energies when they feel lost or bogged down. What can sustain a couple through the most difficult times is knowing that they are together for a larger purpose—helping each other refine the gold of their essential natures by working through obstacles in the way of their deepest unfolding" (8).

Patricia shares that her view of marriage as a path to personal growth sustains her through the difficult times and keeps her faith buoyed atop the stormy waters. Even in the first six months of marriage, when she felt like she was going to die because of her sense of feeling trapped in the relationship, she knew that she and Peter were brought together for a higher purpose. She beautifully articulated her views on the wedding and marriage:

The journey of getting married and being married has been so different than I ever would have imagined. Peter and I both hold the view that marriage is not just to have fun or to have kids, but it's something that helps us evolve on a spiritual level. It is as important a vocation as it is to be a religious person. Supposedly, in the ideal sense, the married couple is evidence of God's love in the world. Someone said that being married is a crucible, and I think that is very true. We feel like in being married each of us is helping the other to strip away the ego. All of our issues are coming up and we are learning, in some fundamental way, how to be less selfish and more loving. We very much see a spiritual purpose behind this whole thing and believe that is why we are together.

There is no doubt that issues will surface in the course of a marriage. These issues could be psychological and emotional—confronting the ways in which we attempt to control or feel controlled, coming to terms with our fears of abandonment and suffocation—and they could be ways that the external world creates obstacles—issues around money, work, living environment, illness, death. If we enter marriage with the belief that we will "live happily ever after," each time a challenge arises we will view it as a problem that we must get rid of. If, on the other hand, we accept that part of the function of marriage is to learn more about ourselves and others, to become more loving and fulfilled people in the world, then each difficult situation becomes an opportunity for growth. Brian, married seventeen years, offered this wisdom when asked what he would say to couples entering marriage:

Be aware that marriage will bring up some of the toughest issues you'll ever have to look at, and that that's a gift, not a burden or something to be avoided. Recognize that conflict is a blessing in disguise, and that it is through resolution of conflict that peace comes. And the greater the conflict, the greater the peace and joy. Be compassionate with yourself and your partner. Recognize that marriage is the most sacred and complex of all interpersonal relationships.

Viewed in this light, marriage becomes a spiritual path. Woman and man are bound to one another the way a nun is bound to her convent and a monk is bound to his monastery. Like the nun and monk, who take vows upon entering their spiritual dwelling, so the married couple take vows upon entering the sacred union of marriage. The vows are a covenant that ask the married couple to abide by certain laws, abstain from certain behaviors, and hike the arduous terrain of their souls as they continually learn what it means to love themselves and another. Marriage is a mature, rigorous discipline. It is also a glorious, rewarding path, for the fruits of this labor are to find one's true nature and to share life with someone who intimately knows the tiny paths of your soul.

Examining Our Expectations

The confusion sets in when we notice that, despite the relatively recent changes in relations between the sexes, men and women still approach each other with expectations of what their partner is going to provide and fulfill. Without the obvious divisions of labor—I'll do the fishing if you fry the fish—the expectations with which we enter marriage become more difficult to recognize. To some extent, most of us enter marriage with the unspoken, and usually unconscious, expectation that our partner will be the answer to our problems, our salvation, our freedom, the missing piece to our puzzle. Even if we are both engaged in purposeful work and both in touch with our inner world, we still carry the legacy of the old marriage model that says, "You will complete me." And in the first months or years of a relationship, this expectation may be fulfilled. Falling in love does create a temporary reprieve from the normal struggles that inform all of our lives. The problems arise when the "love drug" wears off and the simple act of being with our spouse no longer lifts us out of our daily struggles. At this point, the illusion is shattered. Where we once ran toward our partner saying, unconsciously, "You are the answer to my problems!," couples in the early years often find themselves running *away* from their partner, thinking, quite consciously, "You *are* my problem." When we notice that we have fallen into this trap, that is the time for an honest examination of the expectations we each carry concerning the piece we think our partner will fulfill. As Mikael said:

About four years into my marriage I realized that I had been carrying resentment toward Sophia because she was failing to meet my expectations of what a "good" wife was. A good wife was supposed to be a gracious hostess, provide a loving, harmonious, peaceful home environment, be cordial and courteous to my work associates, offer sound business advice, welcome me when I came home from work with a kiss and a hot meal and, on top of all that, provide an exciting sex life! I can see now how backwards that list is, but it was the list that I carried into the marriage without even realizing it. Lately I have started to see that, almost from the moment I met her, I superimposed these expectations onto her, so that when I related to her I wasn't really seeing her but rather who I thought she should be. A lot has changed since I have begun to let go of these expectations and realize that ultimately I need to provide many of those things for myself. I am learning what it means to really love Sophia and not some idea of what a wife is supposed to be.

It is not an easy task to uncover our expectations. As Mikael shared, they are often buried in our unconscious, inherited from the role-modeling of our parents and other important adult figures in our lives. Sometimes it takes several years for a deeply rooted belief to surface, as Brian and Beth discovered. Fifteen years into their marriage, Beth realized that she had not been looking at Brian as a person but as an image of what he would provide. She also became aware of the ways in which she conformed to Brian's image of how she was supposed to behave. Alongside their spoken wedding vows lived a host of unspoken agreements about the ways in which they would fill in each other's holes. When Beth became unhappy in the marriage and withdrew her side of the pact, Brian was devastated. Where was his wife who was there to make him feel better and take care of him emotionally? The two entered a year-long period of intense struggle, where Brian was seriously contemplating whether or not he wanted to remain married. Beth talked about her side of events:

When we married there was an expectation that we were supposed to complete each other. An image was given to me that we were like a puzzle and where you have pieces missing the other person will fill them in. I believed that, so clearly if I'm hurting somewhere it's his job to fix it, and it was my job to do that for him. We did a pretty good job of that for several years! The message was that if we loved each other we would do this filling. At one point, about three years ago, I realized that it wasn't loving for me or for him to continue in the patterns of trying to fill him up and asking to be filled up. I just didn't want to play anymore. We had agreed mutually to this, but I was changing. I told him I didn't want to do that anymore and he had no idea what I was talking about. He was furious with me and there was a long time where I didn't know if he was going to stay or leave. It was the most desperate time in our marriage.

Brian filled in his pieces:

Before I married Beth I had this idea that when I married her life would be heaven. I would be able to take this feeling I had felt with her in our early months of courtship—of completeness and wholeness and euphoria—

and have it forever. I believed for a long time that marriage was the vehicle that was designed to bring me a sense of fullness. When that feeling wore off I thought that there was something wrong with the marriage, that she wasn't the right person for me. What I clearly knew was that this feeling of euphoria I had been looking for wasn't there at all. And I was miserable in a lot of respects. I was miserable in the sense that I kept thinking it was Beth's responsibility to fill me up. When I wasn't satisfied emotionally, sexually, spiritually, occupationally, or mentally I always thought it was someone else's fault. I began to conclude that there was something wrong with our marriage, or with Beth. It was a lot easier to focus on the marriage and on Beth because I wasn't in a place to start taking responsibility for myself. Over time my frustration with my lack of fulfillment reached a critical point and I was ready to leave. I was literally on my way out of the marriage when a book fell into my hands that changed my life. My major breakthrough came when I realized how in virtually every relationship I had, I was looking to the relationship as a means of taking or getting something from someone else rather than giving. I wanted everyone else, mostly Beth, to make my pain go away.

Brian and Beth each came to realize that the way they were approaching their marriage was not working. As Brian learned how to fulfill himself emotionally and spiritually and Beth learned how to put herself first so that her loving actions for Brian were motivated by a genuine desire to give as opposed to a need to please, their marriage transformed dramatically. The expectation that the function of marriage was to fulfill the other partner had proved detrimental to their relationship. Now they both view marriage as the most sacred of all relationships, a daily opportunity to express love and grow as individuals. They came to realize that it is not the relationship with the other person that creates the sense of well-being, but that the well-being exists within each person and it is the challenge as individuals to learn how to access this inner peace. Then the marriage, instead of becoming the vehicle through which each partner is trying to get fulfilled, becomes the place where two individuals learn about themselves and the obstacles that bar the way from becoming more loving, purposeful people in the world. Where it was once an illusory "answer" and then a source of discontent, it is now a place of nourishment and creativity. As Beth said:

Loving Brian is an expression of who I am. I believe that marriage is designed to require the very deepest in us, and to require complete commitment and devotion. It is also designed to give the greatest joy that we can have in this life.

And Brian:

The sense of fullness I have now is far richer and more solid than the sense I had when I was falling in love. When I was falling in love I was only happy when I was with the other person. Now I believe that the sense of euphoria must come from within each individual and that the relationship is the medium where that euphoria, love, and creativity can be expressed with one another.

A Creative Endeavor

Each marriage is a unique relationship that requires constant commitment, courage, and creativity to maintain its vitality. A marriage, like a baby, is a particular configuration of two distinct personalities, a relationship that is born on the wedding day and continues to grow for a lifetime. As we stand on the threshold of creating the new paradigms for healthy marriages, we can remind ourselves that we are pioneers setting out on an exciting road, one never before undertaken. On this fresh terrain there are few footprints we can follow—which can be daunting in that we don't know where to look for inspiration and guidance, but can also be liberating in that we are being handed an opportunity to create a marriage specifically tailored to suit our individual selves. As we come to realize that the old models are outdated and we have not yet developed the new paradigms, we realize that we are, as a generation, in the liminal phase of the relationship between the sexes. The liminal, as we learned through the wedding process, is the in-between time where nothing and everything exist simultaneously. With regard to marriage, we are standing on shifting ground, which will inevitably lead to instability as we find our way. However, we are also in the midst of profound possibility. Our generation carries the mixed blessing of creating a new paradigm for marriage. It is an awesome task.

Each day is an opportunity to reaffirm your vows or create new vows as the marriage evolves. Each day is an opportunity to choose consciously that yes, this is my life partner, and today I choose to share my life with my beloved spouse. Each day is an opportunity to examine honestly what is working and what is not working in the marriage, an opportunity to have courage to plunge into our own selves and discover where we may be contributing to the conflicts. Simply put, each day is an opportunity to express and receive love, and an opportunity to explore the ways in which we are preventing ourselves from loving. As we stand on this threshold, we know that there is no right or wrong way to have a marriage, no standard against which to compare ourselves. There is only your marriage, and the unique ways that you and your partner learn how to walk through this life together.

A Love Letter

I would like to close with a beautiful letter that provided much inspiration and vision as I prepared to marry. It was written to me by a very wise man, Stanley Joy Waxman, married to his beloved Rena for fifty-three years. In the months before my wedding, feeling bereft of positive role models for healthy, passionate, long-term marriages, my best friend, Jessica Williams, compiled a folder of "Marital Inspirations" as part of my shower gift. The folder included letters written to me by married couples whose passion for one another had not only remained steady for at least twenty-five years but, in many cases, had intensified. The letter written by Jessica's grandfather particularly touched me. I include it here as a vision of hope as we all embark on this great, exciting journey called marriage.

Dear Sheryl,

With a dear friend's excitement, Jessica has informed us of your forthcoming marriage. We're delighted with this announcement and hasten to congratulate you and your beloved upon taking this life-shaping step.

It makes us think about our marriage fifty-three years ago; it makes us wonder how we've been able to sustain as a couple throughout that length of time; it makes us try to analyze the ingredients that make for a successful and lasting union.

We conclude that one can't rationalize too much or too well about all this because emotion and instinct play a greater part in the mix and these are not easily pinpointed, labeled, or defined.

We conclude though that it reduces itself simply . . . to LOVE . . . beginning with that certain physical attraction, proceeding to admiration for mind and temperament and soul (if that's not too out-of-

date a concept) and finding that kind of comfortableness, understanding, and intimacy that no other person can provide.

A love that has passion and sensuality and breathless anticipation in it, such as is expressed in The Song of Songs in the Old Testament: "Hark, my beloved! / behold, he cometh, / Leaping upon the mountains, skipping upon the hills . . . "

A love that is constant and well-fixed and is not enticed away. See Shakespeare's Sonnet CXVI . . . "Let me not to the marriage of true minds admit impediments" etc. He put it well.

A love that recognizes each partner's individuality. About this Kahlil Gibran wisely said: " . . . stand together yet not too near together. For the pillars of the temple stand apart, / and the oak tree and the cyprus grow not in each other's shadow."

A love that is ever-mindful of the other, that regards the other as oneself, that puts ego aside and feels a pride that overcomes envy. Erich Fromm put it in a way that has served as a constant reminder to us: "Love," he wrote, "is the active concern for the life and growth of that which we love."

Some of the ingredients of marriage, we believe, are tolerance . . . taking time to understand . . . an ongoing sense of humor . . . a willingness to give and take in good spirit . . . to sense the rhythms of the dance and glide in perfect harmony. A recognition that the road is not always smooth, that the outside world invades and creates twists and turns and throws up roadblocks. But, keeping a practical sense and an honest facing-up as a team can serve to get through those obstacles. To care for, as well as about, one's mate goes a long way toward making it through any storm.

Now one can't really transmit one's own experience or put others in our shoes because all shoes are unique and those who put on their own marital footwear must create their own "last" that will serve their "sole-mates" best (if you'll permit some pretty bad yet not unmeaningful puns). In other words, the only model for success is the model the couple creates for themselves—the patterns of behavior that a twosome lays out, shaped out of mutual wishes, dreams, and aspirations and consonant with their respective temperaments.

What we can convey with assurance—out of our experience—is that the rewards of a life lived fully together, with perpetual excitement in each other's accomplishments, in mutual support at times of failure or stress; a life where there's a strong working together, growing together, a laughing together and sometimes a crying together . . . where the love is tenderly tended and the garden kept green always . . . provides unequaled lifelong satisfaction. These are the riches to be mined.

We wish you both to have in your own way what we have had in ours—the blessings that we know are possible in a marriage entered into with good sense and sensibility, fed by a passion that may diminish but will never be extinguished, undergirded with a love that is capable of growing and strengthening with the years.

Recommended Reading

Johnson, Robert. *She: Understanding Feminine Psychology.* 1989. New York: Harper and Row. A bride's journey to consciousness and wholeness as seen through the myth of Psyche and Eros.

Lerner, Harriet G. *The Dance of Intimacy: A Woman's Guide to Courageous Acts of Change in Key Relationships.* 1989. New York: Harper and Row. An excellent discussion in chapter 12 on the mother-daughter relationship.

Paul, Jordan and Margaret Paul. *Do I Have to Give up Me to be Loved by You?* 1983. Minneapolis, Minn.: CompCare Publishers. How to love another without giving up one's self.

Wallerstein, Judith and Sandra Blakeslee. *The Good Marriage: How and Why Love Lasts.* 1995. New York: Warner Books. Chapter 3 explores the importance of separating from one's family of origin in the early years of marriage.

Wells, Rebecca. *The Divine Secrets of the Ya-Ya Sisterhood*. 1997. New York: HarperCollins Publishers. A beautiful story of how a woman's impending wedding sets her on a journey of unraveling the complexities of the mother-daughter relationship.

Welwood, John. *Love and Awakening: Discovering the Sacred Path of Intimate Relationships*. 1996. New York: Harper-Collins Publishers. Marriage as a spiritual relationship.

Woodman, Marion. *Addiction to Perfection: The Still Unravished Bride*. 1982. Toronto: Inner City Books.

Woodman, Marion. *The Pregnant Virgin: A Process of Psychological Transformation*. 1985. Toronto: Inner City Books. Transition and rites of passage in modern culture.

Woolger, Roger and Jennifer Barker Woolger. *The Goddess Within: A Guide to the Eternal Myths That Shape Women's Lives*. 1987. New York: Ballantine Books. An in-depth look at the Persephone archetype.

Notes

Chapter One

p. 12, *Through studying various groups:* A. van Gennep, *The rites of passage* (Chicago: The University of Chicago Press, 1960), p. 3.

p. 15, *Psychoanalyst Marion Woodman:* M. Woodman, *The pregnant virgin: A process of psychological transformation* (Toronto: Inner City Books, 1985), p. 24.

Chapter Two

p. 42, *Judith Wallerstein:* J. Wallerstein and S. Blakeslee, *The good marriage: How and why love lasts* (New York: Warner Books, 1995), p. 56.

p. 52, *Referring to the bride's journey:* J. Wallerstein and S. Blakeslee, *The good marriage: How and why love lasts* (New York: Warner Books, 1995), p. 55.

p. 62, *Bruce Lincoln in:* B. Lincoln, *Emerging from the chrysalis* (Cambridge, MA: Harvard University Press, 1981), p. 79.

p. 66, *Robert Johnson noted:* R. Johnson, *She: Understanding feminine psychology* (New York: Harper and Row, 1989), p. 17.

Chapter Three

p. 85, *Because she receives:* M. Woodman, *The ravished bridegroom* (Toronto: Inner City Books, 1990), p. 160.

p. 85, *Two such tales:* J. Godwin and A. McLean (commentary), *The chemical wedding of Christian Rosenkreutz* (Grand Rapids, MI: Phanes Press, 1991).

p. 89, *But brides should ponder:* M. Woodman, *Addiction to perfection: The still unravished bride* (Toronto: Inner City Books, 1982), p. 50.

p. 90, *As Joseph Campbell writes:* J. Campbell, *The hero with a thousand faces* (Princeton, NJ: Princeton University Press, 1949), p. 28.

p. 94, *A book on overcoming*: L. Bassett, *From panic to power* (New York: HarperCollins, Publishers, Inc, 1995), p. 63.

Chapter Five

p. 144, *Martin Buber wrote on:* M. Buber,*Tales of the Hasidim* (New York: Schocken, 1947), p. 104.

p. 148, *Robert Johnson, referring:* R. Johnson, *She: Understanding feminine psychology* (New York: Harper and Row, 1989), p. 50.

p. 154, *About the last category he says*: A. van Gennep,*The rites of passage* (Chicago: The University of Chicago Press, 1960), p. 29.

p. 155, *The threshold symbolizes:* J. Campbell, *The hero with a thousand faces* (Princeton, NJ: Princeton University Press, 1949), p. 51.

Chapter Six

p. 176, *Psychologist F.F. Flach:* F.F. Flach, *The Secret Strength of Depression* (New York: J.B. Lippincott, 1974), p. 31.

p. 176, *Leah Heidenrich, in her Master's thesis:* L. Heidenrich, *Bride Illusion: Depression in newlywed women* (Unpublished master's thesis, Carpinteria, CA: Pacifica Graduate Institute, 1990.

p. 176, *Heidenrich wrote:* L. Heidenrich, ibid, p. 68.

Chapter Seven

p. 201,*Welwood in:* J. Welwood, *Love and Awakening* (New York: Harper Collins, 1996), p. 8.

References

Bassett, Lucinda. 1995. *From Panic to Power*. New York: HarperCollins.

Births, Marriages, Divorces, and Deaths for 1996. (July, 1997). Monthly Vital Statistics Report, 45 (12), 1.

Buber, Martin. 1947. *Tales of the Hasidim*. New York: Schocken.

Campbell, Joseph. 1949. *The Hero with a Thousand Faces*. Princeton, N.J.: Princeton University Press.

Flach, Frederic. 1974. *The Secret Strength of Depression*. New York: J.B. Lippincott.

Godwin, Joscelyn and Adam McLean. 1991. Commentary, *The Chemical Wedding of Christian Rosenkreutz*. Grand Rapids, Mich.: Phanes Press.

Heidenrich, Leah. 1990. *Bride Illusion: Depression in Newly-wed Women*. Unpublished master's thesis. Carpinteria, Calif.: Pacifica Graduate Institute.

Hendricks, Kathlyn and Gay Hendricks. 1997. *The Conscious Heart*. New York: Bantam Books.

Johnson, Robert. 1989. *She: Understanding Feminine Psychology*. New York: Harper and Row.

Lincoln, Bruce. 1981. *Emerging from the Chrysalis*. Cambridge, Mass.: Harvard University Press.

Van Gennep, Arnold. 1960. *The Rites of Passage*. Chicago: The University of Chicago Press.

Wallerstein, Judith and Sandra Blakeslee. 1995. *The Good Marriage: How and Why Love Lasts*. New York: Warner Books.

Welwood, John. 1996. *Love and Awakening*. New York: HarperCollins.

Woodman, Marion. 1982. *Addiction to Perfection: The Still Unravished Bride*. Toronto: Inner City Books

Woodman, Marion. 1985. *The Pregnant Virgin: A Process of Psychological Transformation*. Toronto: Inner City Books.

Woodman, Marion. 1990. *The Ravished Bridegroom*. Toronto: Inner City Books.

Zukav, Gary. 1989. *The Seat of the Soul*. New York: Fireside.

Acknowledgments

I would like to express my warm and loving thanks to:

My mom, Margaret Paul, for showing me the way.

My grandparents, Charlotte and Izzy Brustein, for supporting me through several schools, but mostly through the school of life.

Jessica (Bes) Williams, my soul mate, my shining star, my mother, my sister, my best friend, my editor, my voice, my solace.

Carrie Dinow, my soul-sister and bookend, whose irreplaceable light and depth are infinite gifts in my life.

Lisa Suneson, Danielle Ray, Donna Gorman, Jamie Nagler, Lawrence Monoson, Steve Leeds, Tommy Jordan, and the entire Paul clan, true friends and family who continually support, reflect, and inspire.

Jim Hosney at Crossroads School, who opened the door that invited words from another realm to enter.

Catharine Sutker at New Harbinger Publications, an acquisitions editor from heaven who made the experience of birthing this book nothing but pleasurable.

New Harbinger Publications for their commitment to publishing books that promote well-being and consciousness.

Roy Carlisle for all of his encouragement along the way.

My writer-guides—Marion Woodman, Robert Johnson, Alice Walker, Carl Jung, Gary Zukav—and my poet-guides—Rumi, Rilke, Whitman, Dickinson, Neruda—for showing me who I am and who I am becoming.

Finally, my gratitude to the Creative Source, the guiding principle in my life.

More Women Talk About Titles

JUICY TOMATOES

A diverse group of women join in a tell-all conversation about what it really takes to thrive after 50 that serves as a support group, a handbook, and a chorus of supportive friends, all rolled up into one.

Item JTOM $13.95

UNDER HER WING

Dozens of women who have enjoyed a mentor-protégé relationship help you get beyond fears that have kept you from reaching out to other women and initiate and maintain a successful mentoring relationship.

Item WING $13.95

AFTER THE BREAKUP

Straight, lesbian, and bisexual women of all ages speak out about what really happens when couplehood ends and offer fresh perspectives on how to rebuild your identity and enjoy a life filled with new possibilities.

Item ATB $13.95

FACING 30

A diverse group of women who are either teetering on the brink of 30 or have made it past the big day talk about careers, relationships, the inevitable kid question, and dashed dreams.

Item F30 $12.95

CLAIMING YOUR CREATIVE SELF

Shares the inspiring stories of women who were able to keep in touch with their creative spirit and let it lead them to a place in their lives where something truly magical is taking place.

Item CYCS $15.95

GOODBYE GOOD GIRL

Dozens of women confirm that it may be scary to challenge the rules that dictate what a woman can be and do, but the results can be astonishing, inspiring, and well worth the struggle.

Item GGG $12.95

Call **toll-free 1-800-748-6273** to order. Have your Visa or Mastercard number ready. Or send a check for the titles you want to New Harbinger Publications, 5674 Shattuck Avenue, Oakland, CA 94609. Include $4.50 for the first book and 75¢ for each additional book to cover shipping and handling. (California residents please include appropriate sales tax.) Allow four to six weeks for delivery.

Prices subject to change without notice.

Some Other New Harbinger Titles

Sex Talk, Item SEXT $12.95

Everyday Adventures for the Soul, Item EVER $11.95

A Woman's Addiction Workbook, Item $18.95

The Daughter-In-Law's Survival Guide, Item DSG $12.95

PMDD, Item PMDD $13.95

The Vulvodynia Survival Guide, Item VSG $15.95

Love Tune-Ups, Item LTU $10.95

The Deepest Blue, Item DPSB $13.95

The 50 Best Ways to Simplify Your Life, Item FWSL $11.95

Brave New You, Item BVNY $13.95

Loving Your Teenage Daughter, Item LYTD $14.95

The Hidden Feelings of Motherhood, Item HFM $14.95

The Woman's Book of Sleep, Item WBS $14.95

Pregnancy Stories, Item PS $14.95

The Women's Guide to Total Self-Esteem, Item WGTS $13.95

Thinking Pregnant, Item TKPG $13.95

The Conscious Bride, Item CB $12.95

Juicy Tomatoes, Item JTOM $13.95

Facing 30, Item F30 $12.95

The Money Mystique, Item MYST $13.95

High on Stress, Item HOS $13.95

Perimenopause, 2nd edition, Item PER2 $16.95

Call **toll free, 1-800-748-6273,** or log on to our online bookstore at **www.newharbinger.com** to order. Have your Visa or Mastercard number ready. Or send a check for the titles you want to New Harbinger Publications, Inc., 5674 Shattuck Ave., Oakland, CA 94609. Include $4.50 for the first book and 75¢ for each additional book, to cover shipping and handling. (California residents please include appropriate sales tax.) Allow two to five weeks for delivery.

Prices subject to change without notice.